MEMOIRS FROM THE
MARKETPLACE

MEMOIRS FROM THE
MARKETPLACE

30 Homilies to
Better Understand God's Love

Dr. Richard L. Hamlet

Global Ministries Foundation
Cordova, Tennessee

Memoirs from the Marketplace

Global Ministries Foundation
65 Germantown Ct., Ste. 409
Cordova, TN 38018

Library of Congress Control Number: 2022900782

ISBN: 978-1-949856-61-3 (paperback)
ISBN: 978-1-949856-62-0 (e-book)

1 2 3 4 5—26 25 24 23 22

DEDICATION

· · ✦ ✦ ✦ ✦ ✦ · ·

To the wife of my youth, Ginger Hamlet, and
my daughter, Natalie Metcalf, for their steadfast support
and hard work supporting me

CONTENTS

···✦✦✦···

PREFACE

···✦✦✦···

*D*ear friend, years ago when I worked as a financial professional in the capital markets as a Wall Street–trained practitioner, God placed a growing burden in my soul regarding the spiritual posture of many whom I encountered who had achieved much material and financial success in their respective vocations. I began to observe closely those in the "marketplace," both employees and employers, with regard to both their work ethic and priorities of life. For the purposes of this book, I use the term *marketplace* to refer to the daily activities of believers in Christ within their relationships, wherever they go, and whomever they meet. Very broad, yet all believers have a unique platform of influence in which they can be faithful anointed witnesses for Christ.

It became clear to me that the marketplace was an arena where the vast majority of constituents knew very little of the biblical gospel of Jesus Christ and His redemptive work for fallen human beings. Years later, after the Lord called me into the pastorate as a minister of the gospel, this burden did not go away. In fact, the burden intensified as I saw the lostness of many "outside the church walls" who may never enter into a church worship service or otherwise hear the proclamation of the gospel in a formal public assembly.

Thus, it became apparent that if Christ's church, the redeemed of the Lord, were going to have an impact on leading these constituents to Christ, then there must be a renewed emphasis on the biblical mandate of the Great Commission of Jesus. The intentional, prayerful, and bold witness of Christians in the marketplace is nothing new to this generation. However, the challenge from Scripture must be embraced by every generation with regard to every believer taking "ownership" of their privilege and responsibility to share the good news to those they encounter on a daily basis.

This is the background for the book. This collection of "Homilies," which are really defined as short messages, spring from a national radio program I have hosted for the past several years titled *Ministry in the Marketplace* (MITM). My prayer is that as you read this book the Holy Spirit will challenge and empower you from the truths explained and amplified from Scripture in each chapter. God is in the business of using ordinary Christians to be extraordinary gospel witnesses through the power of the Holy Spirit living in them.

May God in His grace use you, dear friend, to be that witness for Jesus.

Richard L. Hamlet

DAY 1

· · + + ◆ + + · ·

And they ate of the produce of the land on the day after the Passover, unleavened bread and parched grain, on the very same day. Then the manna ceased on the day after they had eaten the produce of the land; and the children of Israel no longer had manna, but they ate the food of the land of Canaan that year.

Joshua 5:11–12

*T*he people of God had wandered for forty years in the wilderness. The book of Exodus teaches about the judgment of the people because of their rebellion and unbelief. But in the book of Joshua, we see a new day. In these verses, we see God was granting the opportunity for a new generation of believers to go into the land of promise, the land of milk and honey promised to Abraham.

I tell you our God is faithful, and no matter how dark a generation becomes, how dark a culture or society, God is a faithful covenant-keeping God. I want to share three observations that flow out of these verses dealing with Joshua as the leader of God's people during this time.

I tell you our God is faithful, and no matter how dark a generation becomes, how dark a culture or society, God is a faithful covenant-keeping God.

This was a new day. The Old Covenant provided two important acts of obedience by the people of God, (1) circumcision and (2) the celebration of the Passover. Both essential Old Testament rituals were neglected when the people of God left Egypt and wandered in the wilderness. There was a need for restoration around the Word of God. There was a need for God's people to come in obedience again. This new generation, born in the wilderness or under twenty years old in Egypt when they crossed the Red Sea, were now being led by Joshua and Caleb into the land of promise. The first thing they did was obey these two Old Covenant commands. Those who were uncircumcised were circumcised.

Next, they celebrated the Passover, the memorial meal that God instituted in Exodus when the Angel of Death passed over those faithful Hebrews who placed the blood of the unblemished lamb on their doorpost. It was a new day—a new day for this new generation, and they began by obedience to the Word of God. Today as God raises up a new generation within every society and culture, the gospel must remain relevant. It is not enough to say, "Oh, let's look back and see what God has done in the past." God is not only the God of the past, but He is the God of the present and the God of the future. Jesus Christ is the same yesterday, today, and forever. The God of Israel is the God of the Bible who continues to raise up individuals like you and me to minister in the marketplace by taking the gospel to the ends of the earth. It was a new day for these Israelites as they crossed over and began their conquest within the land of promise.

Secondly, not only was there a new day but *there was also a new diet.* The Israelites had eaten manna for many years in the wilderness. God was faithful, but they had the same food every day for forty years. Can you imagine the exhilaration, the enthusiasm when a new day came, and they crossed the River Jordan? They entered the Promised Land and began eating from the crops of the field. They began to eat from the land of milk and honey, and they began feasting on the crops. Can you imagine that transformation? The Israelites began to have a full diet. They began to experience the abundance of wonderful blessings from God.

Today our society needs a new diet. Those outside of Christ must be born again because they have never tasted or seen that the Lord is gracious. As Christ's church, we need to pray God would expand our diet, and through that, we would partake of the gospel. The faith in our lives will allow it to be an outreach within the sphere of influence God has given us. We are blessed with so many restaurants in the United States. There are so many places to eat and almost too many choices to make. Today we need to go from drinking spiritual milk to eating spiritual meat.

Our people need a renewed enthusiasm for knowing that God gives us a purpose to go into the marketplace. We are to go as salt and light and be dependent upon God to empower us to be change agents within our culture and society. If there has ever been a need for a new diet, a true gospel-centered spiritual diet, it is now. May that begin in you and me.

Finally, not only was it a new day with the people of God, not only a new diet, but *God gave them a new direction.* They began to prepare for the conquest right after this verse. Within the context of Scripture, Joshua sees the angel of the Lord, who is the captain of the army of God. He bows before him. This shows us that this angel was an angel of the Lord God Himself. There seemed to be a new direction that God gave Joshua as the leader of His people, but really it was not. It was a direction God had given Abraham before. Still, this generation needed to see their identity—to see their place in God's mission in terms of His redemptive plan for mankind and within the people of Israel. And so, there was a renewed direction.

Can you imagine that a three-day journey from Egypt to Canaan took forty years because of disobedience, rebellion, and unbelief? It is almost like running on a treadmill and going nowhere. Can you imagine that new direction and seeing how God opened the door for this new, younger generation to be able to see God's promises fulfilled with their own eyes?

Joshua would go forth as the leader. It was a great conquest where they were no longer going in circles but were headed now in a new direction. It was a beeline, and it was a beeline that was in the epicenter of God's redemptive plan. They would march forth, with the first conquest being Jericho. They went forward and God began to give them the promised inheritance as they were faithful and obedient to His Word in their generation. May our generation see that time is short and be assured Jesus is coming back soon. There is never a "more perfect" time for kingdom influence in the marketplace than now.

God bless you, my friend.

DAY 2

· · ◆ ◆ ◆ ◆ · ·

Therefore the king said to me, "Why is your face sad, since you are not sick? This is nothing but sorrow of heart."

So I became dreadfully afraid, and said to the king, "May the king live forever! Why should my face not be sad, when the city, the place of my fathers' tombs, lies waste, and its gates are burned with fire?"

Nehemiah 2:2–3

The book of Nehemiah is a book of history in the Old Testament. Nehemiah was a government official in Persia, the world power of the time. Simply put, his position was similar to the chief of staff to the king of Persia. This was a time when Jerusalem had been destroyed by the Babylonians years before. There was much debris and decay, what we would call "blight" today. That was the condition of the City of David, Jerusalem. In chapter 1, we see that the Lord stirred in Nehemiah. He became greatly stressed when he heard a report of the condition of the decay of Jerusalem, so he went to the king. In this text, we see his time of intercession before the most powerful human being in the world at the time, the king of Persia. There are three observations I want to share with you in these two verses of Nehemiah. I want you to see his sorrow, his strategy, and his strength.

First, notice when Nehemiah walked in to perform his role as the cupbearer, the king immediately saw his countenance was full of sorrow. In other words, he was physically sick. You know, it is never fun being sick. In our country today, we are blessed to have many types of medical treatment and prescription drugs. Nehemiah did not have those during his day, but we know what it is like to be sick. Generally, sickness comes from something ingested into our body or something in our cells or bloodstream. None of those things were the reason why Nehemiah was sick. Nehemiah was sick because God put in his heart that the city of Jerusalem, what many call the City of God, had now been destroyed. It needed to be rebuilt.

In other words, the marketplace there in Jerusalem was decimated. God placed a vision on Nehemiah's heart to go back and rebuild the city's gates and the walls. It was time for revitalization in that marketplace. Has there been a time in your life when you were literally sick or maybe physically or mentally disturbed because you were burdened by seeing the onslaught of wickedness in your community? You can identify with Nehemiah today if that is the case because all was not well. Instead, all was dark, and he wanted to be used of God to be a light within God's visible community, the Jewish congregation, as they were reassembling in Jerusalem after Zerubbabel had rebuilt the temple. First of all, I want you to see his sorrow. It was real, and Paul expressed in his epistles that he had a feeling of sorrow for the darkness in the world. Friend, our prayer today should be that God's kingdom will come on earth as it is in heaven. We should pray that God, who is the God of restoration, the God of second chances, the God of revitalization, will have a sorrow that is not a sorrow of man through His gospel,

His people, and His church. Hear me, that we would have a feeling of godly sorrow, that things are not right.

We should pray that God, who is the God of restoration, the God of second chances, the God of revitalization, will have a sorrow that is not a sorrow of man through His gospel, His people, and His church.

Second, *if we are going to have that sorrow from God, then we need to have His strategy.* Nehemiah had a strategy of going back to Jerusalem. As a leader, Nehemiah took a team and went to rebuild Jerusalem. He had a plan, and his strategy was one of godly wisdom. No doubt he would have prayed as James prayed. "If any of you lacks wisdom, let him ask of God" (James 1:5). He understood he needed the wisdom to strategize, execute, and accomplish the work of God in rebuilding the physical kingdom within the city of Jerusalem. He had a strategy. In all of our worldwide travels, over seventy countries, I have seen many different cultures and many decimated communities. I have seen much blight. I want to tell you, though, that the physical decimation in blight does not come close to the significant level of spiritual blight, darkness, and rebellion around the world. There are many in different cultures today going about their daily lives without any strategy to reach those outside the gospel of Jesus Christ.

Last, we can think about his strength. What was it that kept him going? We can fast forward to Nehemiah 8.

Nehemiah and Ezra were having a great worship service with a heaven-sent revival, celebrating the finishing of the wall in fifty-two days, and oh how God was glorified. There is a portion of verse 10 that stands out. Nehemiah simply says, "the joy of the LORD is your strength." This is what we want to leave you with today, that God will give you a feeling of sorrow for the lost world around you in the marketplace. We pray that God will give you the strategy, and you will look to others for counsel on how you can be effective within your domain and culture, within your workplace, and within your family to advance the gospel of Jesus Christ. What you need is that strength of the Lord.

I need the strength of the Lord because the world, the flesh, and the devil seek to delay us and distract us, to divert us from advancing the kingdom of God in our own lives and our own marketplace. The joy of the Lord comes from Jesus Himself, Christ in you and me. The hope of glory is not only for the next world. It is for our world and our life today. We must have Christ in us before He can live in and through us. Nehemiah was a leader in his society, but God had placed a burden on him that his most important role was to advance the kingdom of God here on earth, as it is in heaven.

God bless you, my friend.

DAY 3

···✦✦✦✦···

But when he came to himself, he said, "How many of my father's hired servants have bread enough and to spare, and I perish with hunger! I will arise and go to my father, and will say to him, 'Father, I have sinned against heaven and before you, and I am no longer worthy to be called your son. Make me like one of your hired servants.'"

And he arose and came to his father. But when he was still a great way off, his father saw him and had compassion, and ran and fell on his neck and kissed him.

Luke 15:17–20

ere we find the Parable of the Lost Son in chapter 15 of Luke. In addition to the Lost Son, there are two more parables in this chapter: the Lost Sheep and A Little Silver.

A parable is simply an earthly story with a heavenly meaning. In our reading, we pick up in the middle of this parable, and I want to share three words flowing from these verses.

The first word is *rebellion*. There was a wealthy man who owned a business. He had two sons, and the younger son came to the point where he demanded his portion of the father's goods, his life estate.

We know that inheritances and bequests are normally given on a testimony basis at death. For a person to demand their share of an inheritance while the grantor was still alive sends a message. This young man decided he was going to go rogue or go against his father's wishes and intentions and what was customary in terms of family possessions. There came a day when he said, "I want my goods."

Dear friend, hear me today. This is a picture, not only of a young son wanting something from his earthly father that he was not entitled to at that time, but also a picture of you and I as souls of God, our heavenly Father, when we choose to go outside His will. By doing this, we are just like this lost son who rebelled against his earthly father. Someone has said that the national anthem of hell today could be "I Did It My Way."

This is far from humorous. Rather it is sobering because every person who has been born in this world is accountable to God as creator, and only those who by the grace of God realize their rebellion against Him will have the opportunity to be restored.

The next word I would like to point out is *repentance*. We picked up in the reading from verse 17 where this young man has rebelled against his father and is now no longer in his residence where he had grown up and labored within the family business. He was far away from his father's house, and there finally came a day when he understood he had sinned against his father by disobeying his will. By the grace of God, he came to the point of repentance.

The word repentance simply means having godly sorrow. Biblical repentance is when you and I come to the point where we realize that we have offended our loving Creator, and we have disobeyed His revealed will and Word. We come to Him with empty hands and without any excuses or boasting of merit in ourselves. Instead, we cast ourselves upon the gospel mercies in Jesus Christ.

This young man came to the realization that he was working as a hired hand, living in a foreign country where there was famine, and he had no goods, and now he remembers the goodness of his father. Romans 2:4 tells us that the goodness of God leads us to repentance, which means

We come to Him with empty hands and without any excuses or boasting of merit in ourselves. Instead, we cast ourselves upon the gospel mercies in Jesus Christ.

that under the conviction of the Holy Spirit, we see how God is good in all His ways and that our rebellion and sinfulness deserve everlasting punishment. Yet God has, in His goodness, come to us and stirred us and brought us to our senses.

Hear me. In the marketplace, there are so many who have yet to experience the saving grace of Jesus Christ. So many are wrapped deep in their careers, wealth management, and job security, yet are pagans living in a culture where Jesus Christ is no longer proclaimed. You and I have the opportunity as we go into the marketplace and proclaim the good news of Jesus Christ and His gospel.

Like this young man in the parable, many come to that point of repentance by the grace of God and through the Spirit of God. This means a change in attitude and action. It means reversing course. Previously one is on the road to destruction under the wrath of God, but by the grace of God, there is a turning to God, repentance toward Him, and faith in the Lord Jesus Christ. That is what was happening in this young man's life as he came to his senses and saw all that he needed to return to the father's house.

The last word or observation is the word *reconciliation*. Did you see in the passage that the young man confessed his sins and demonstrated that confession and repentance of sin by changing his course and going toward the father? Did you see the father's great love? This parable is called the Parable of the Lost Son. But we could also call it the Parable of the Great Father's Love.

We see a picture of the love of God the Father, as the son's father pursued his son who had left him. The son deserved to be cast out of the family relationship, but as soon as the father saw his son responding to his goodness, he accelerated the pursuit of his son in reconciliation. Second Corinthians 5:19 says, "God was in Christ reconciling the world to Himself, not imputing their trespasses to them [us]." He has provided His gospel grace, in the shed blood of Jesus Christ, to cover us with His imputed righteousness and to reconcile us to Himself. We are no longer castaways. We are no longer prodigals. We returned to the Father in repentance and faith. By His grace, He has reconciled us all along the way.

Oh, this is the beauty of the gospel as this father ran, approaching the son and grabbing and kissing him, and falling on him with compassion.

Dear friend, in the marketplace, in the sanctuaries, in the streets and the stadiums, wherever God's gospel is proclaimed by servants such as you and me, there are those who the Spirit of God convicts and calls to point us to Jesus Christ. Reconciliation is when the barriers of hostility are removed.

Here we see in this parable a picture of God's pursuing grace for hell-bound sinners such as you and me. The marketplace is waiting to hear that God is a reconciling God in the gospel of His Son. May we be His lips in life as we herald the gospel across the street and around the world.

God bless you, my friend.

DAY 4

⋯⋅◆◆◆⋅⋯

So Cornelius said, "Four days ago I was fasting until this hour;
and at the ninth hour I prayed in my house, and behold, a man
stood before me in bright clothing, and said, 'Cornelius, your prayer
has been heard, and your alms are remembered in the sight of God.
Send therefore to Joppa and call Simon here, whose surname is
Peter. He is lodging in the house of Simon, a tanner, by the sea.
When he comes, he will speak to you.' So I sent to you immediately,
and you have done well to come. Now therefore, we are all present
before God, to hear all the things commanded you by God."

Acts 10:30–33

*A*cts is a book of early church history—a narrative about the
church coming from its explosion and growth at Pentecost.
They were completed Jews. There came a day where God
manifested Himself in such a way to show His people that the
gospel was also for the Gentiles. This was a radical thing. We find
in this narrative a Gentile man named Cornelius. Earlier in this
chapter, we find Cornelius had a dream. God gave him a vision to
call for a man named Peter, who was in Joppa. Peter was a leader
in Christ's church, so we find in this scripture a conversation where

Cornelius shared with Peter his desire to hear about the things of God. There are three observations I want to share that flow out of Acts 10 in this narrative concerning Cornelius and Peter.

Our first observation is *Cornelius was a seeker*. If you refer to the beginning of chapter 10, you find him described as a God-fearer, one devout in his religion. Here is a Gentile man obviously exposed to the things of God. He had seen the people of God in Israel, the Jews, and he heard about the God of the Bible. Here he was having a dream, where God came to him in a vision. God told him to find a man named Peter in Joppa and listen to what he had to say. Let me clarify when we say he was a seeker. The Bible says that no man seeks after God in their own intuition (Romans 3:11). "All have sinned and fall short of the glory of God" (v. 23), and only God is good (Mark 10:18). So, the natural man, who is all of us as we are in sin, must be born again by the gospel. This happens when we hear the gospel, repent, and believe in the Lord Jesus Christ.

Cornelius had an incomplete understanding of the things of God. He had an inadequate understanding, but the Bible says that God has revealed Himself to all creation. We call this His general revelation. Romans 1 talks about how each of us has a responsibility to know God through creation, and even through our own conscience. This is the general revelation. My wife and I have traveled to over seventy countries, preaching the gospel, and training national church leaders in ministry. We have seen those who have an incomplete understanding or knowledge about the gospel—even if they have never heard the gospel before. Many times, when a person responds to the light through creation and conscience, God in His grace will give them more light. That light will lead them to the special revelation of Jesus Christ. I believe this is what happened to Cornelius as he was first a seeker. He feared God to the best of his knowledge. He gave alms and prayed. He wanted to call out to God, but he did not yet know Jesus Christ as his Lord and Savior. He needed to hear the gospel, and God was so gracious to use this vision.

Dear friend, around the world today, God is using visions and dreams within unreached people groups. We hear many testimonies from some of our international partners and indigenous people groups of how God is intervening and is supernaturally coming through dreams and visions. However, the dream or vision is not the end. It is simply a way of revealing Jesus Christ or pointing them toward a person who can share the gospel with them. It is an amazing thing.

> **We hear many testimonies from some of our international partners and indigenous people groups of how God is intervening and is supernaturally coming through dreams and visions. However, the dream or vision is not the end. It is simply a way of revealing Jesus Christ or pointing them toward a person who can share the gospel with them. It is an amazing thing.**

The second observation is *Cornelius began as a seeker but moved to an inquirer.* An inquirer is someone who wants to hear about the gospel, but they have not come to the point where they are willing to deny themselves and take up their cross and follow Jesus. He has moved from generally seeking God within his sinful nature to responding to the light of general revelation. God has connected him providentially with this man named Peter, a leader in Christ's church and an apostle of Jesus Christ. While Cornelius had his vision, God was also giving Peter a vision. Peter was an Orthodox Jew and a follower of Christ. He was born again by the gospel but had not abandoned some of his rituals or ceremonial laws of the Old Testament. He needed to hear the truth from God—that the gospel is not only for the Jews and the twelve tribes of Israel, but it is also for the Gentiles. The gospel is for every people group, for every ethnicity.

We find that Peter had a vision from God as well. God spoke both to the unregenerate Gentile and to Peter, the apostle, in a vision. He connected these two visions, and this is where we find Cornelius in this passage. Cornelius wanted to hear what Peter had to say about God. He wanted to hear all the things that God had sent to his household to share. Wow. As an evangelist of our Lord Jesus Christ, when these situations come up in my personal experience—oh, to see those who are coming under conviction of sin and want to hear how they can have their sin removed! That is the work of the Holy Spirit, but the gospel must be proclaimed. No one will ever be swayed without hearing the gospel of Jesus Christ.

In Romans, the apostle Paul said he was a debtor to all men. I believe in the power of the gospel, for it is the power of God to salvation to every man that believes. Here we find Cornelius as an inquirer, open to hearing and responding to a light that God gave him and willing to hear what Peter had to share with him.

This leads us to the third observation. *Cornelius became a convert.* He started as a seeker, became an inquirer, and finally became a convert. Later in this chapter, we see where he heard the gospel from Peter clearly in its simplicity. The Holy Spirit came and did His work of grace, and Cornelius and his household heard the gospel. They made their public professions of faith through believers' baptism. God is an awesome God. He can take someone who is a general seeker of religion or even interested in components of Christianity and transform them. "Therefore, if anyone is in Christ, he is a new creation; old things have passed away; behold, all things have become new" (2 Corinthians 5:17). Cornelius became a new creature *through* repentance toward God and faith in the Lord Jesus Christ.

The marketplace is full of religious people. It is full of the philosophies and the traditions of man, but the gospel of the Lord Jesus is the only way that a man, woman, boy, or girl can be made right with the Holy God. Jesus Christ is the way, the truth, and the life, and none of us can come to God except through faith in Christ (John 14:6). That is what the message was to Cornelius. That is the message we must take to the streets. That is what we must do outside the church walls. Many would never go into a worship center but need someone like you and me to go to them and be obedient like Peter was to the great commission of Jesus Christ.

God bless you, my friend.

DAY 5

···◆◆◆◆◆···

So Gideon and the hundred men who were with him came to the outpost of the camp at the beginning of the middle watch, just as they had posted the watch; and they blew the trumpets and broke the pitchers that were in their hands. Then the three companies blew the trumpets and broke the pitchers—they held the torches in their left hands and the trumpets in their right hands for blowing—and they cried, "The sword of the LORD and of Gideon!" And every man stood in his place all around the camp; and the whole army ran and cried out and fled. When the three hundred blew the trumpets, the Lord set every man's sword against his companion throughout the whole camp; and the army fled to Beth Acacia, toward Zererah, as far as the border of Abel Meholah, by Tabbath.

Judges 7:19–22

Here we are in the Old Testament where we see the history of God's visible community of faith. This was during the time of the judges. God raised up Gideon to be the valiant leader who would deliver the people of God from the oppression of their enemy the Midianites. There are three observations I want to share with you about this pivotal event during God's deliverance of His people from the enemy that oppressed them.

Our first observation is *God's ways are not man's ways.* In the context preceding this passage, God told Gideon to mobilize an army—the army of the Lord, to fight against the Midianites. The army began with thirty-two thousand candidates. Gideon had thirty-two thousand men who wanted to fight. But God told Gideon that there were too many troops, and they needed to whittle the army down. They asked those who were fearful to go back to their homes, and many left. There were still too many soldiers remaining, so God told them to go to a nearby brook and drink. Based on how they drank the water, God chose who would fight in the battle. He whittled the army down from thirty-two hundred to three hundred men. Three hundred men!

God's ways are not our ways. The Midianites were large, and they were overwhelming. They had oppressed God's people, and the Israelites had cried out for a deliverer. God gave them Gideon, anointed with the Spirit of the Lord, who went into this battle expecting God to deliver them.

But let me tell you this. Like you and me, Gideon had to learn as we minister in the marketplace that it must be God's ways and not man's if we are going to advance the kingdom of God.

Our second observation is *God's provision is not man's decision.* These three hundred men were divided into three, one-hundred-man platoons. They had a trumpet in one hand and a pitcher with a lamp inside in the other. "Where was the weapon?" you may ask. That is a good observation, dear friend, but God's provision is not man's decision.

You would think, oh surely, if that were today in our contemporary society within our turf wars or battles, with all our weapons of mass destruction, they would have grenades and a great strategy to go out with detailed attacks, all done with great human

God's provision is a sovereign act. The people of God know not by power and might but by the Spirit of God in their journey. wisdom. But God's provision is not man's decision. There came that time when the people blew the trumpets, and these three hundred men's pitchers broke. They had their lamps, their battle cry, and the sword of the Lord and Gideon.

Oh, dear friend, here we see the sovereignty of God and human responsibility. God's provision is a sovereign act. The people of God know not by power and might but by the Spirit of God in their journey.

Dear friend, today you and I are in the marketplace, and like Gideon, are facing the world, the flesh, and the devil. We are facing Antichrist attacks. We are facing those who do not want us to be salt and light within a darkened world. This world is not getting better, it is getting worse, and the depravity of sin and the opposition to the rule and reign of God's sovereignty is accelerating. But dear friend, God's provision, His grace in the gospel of Jesus Christ, is for you today like it was for Gideon as he led these three hundred men. We need to know there is the sword of the Lord. Yes, that is God's sovereign act of redemption. Listen, there is also the sword of Gideon, which is you and me, filled with the Spirit. Anointed, we go forth in proclamation and practice. You and I have an intentional evangelism—a Great Commission mission to all the ends of the earth as we advance the kingdom of God. I tell you, today we live in a time of great opportunity. The harder those assaults come from hell, the more we need to know it is God's provision, not man's decision in the matter of spiritual warfare.

And our last observation is *God's redemption is not man's invention.* I get excited seeing the ending here because we see God moving, and Gideon's army did not have to raise their hand with one weapon. They did not have to shoot one arrow. They cried out to the

Lord and declared the message of God's redemption, the sword of the Lord, and Gideon. Man will always try to manufacture or construct a way to be right with God. Redemption is something that man seeks in his own sinfulness and his old wickedness. Do you remember those who built the Tower of Babel? They tried to construct a tower that reached into the heavens. They knew God through general revelation in the book of Genesis, but dear friend, they tried to be like God with their human wisdom and human invention. They wanted to reach God in their own efforts.

Since the fall of man with Adam, we are separated from God, and there is only the grace of God, through Jesus Christ, that reconciles us to our Holy Creator. There is nothing that human beings can manufacture or construct. Here we see Gideon with three hundred men going forth and God giving them the victory. God confounds the enemy and those pagans who worshiped idols and rejected the God of the Bible, the Creator of the universe. They came into judgment in a temporal way. They were destroyed, or really, they destroyed themselves.

God's redemption is not man's provision. God does not desire that any should perish but that each and every one would repent of their sins and cast themselves on Jesus Christ. There are those in the marketplace you will work with this week who are outside of Christ. Oh, would you share with them the love of God in Jesus Christ? Would you share with them that Jesus came into the world on a rescue mission? He came to save sinners, and there is no one so sinful that the grace of God cannot save them if they will repent of their sins.

Oh, the Holy Spirit must do a work of grace. No man can create or manufacture a saving path, but the grace of God, which brings salvation, has appeared to all men and anyone who will come to God through faith in Jesus Christ and forsake their sins. That is God's redemption, but it is not man's invention.

God bless you, my friend.

DAY 6

·····◆◆◆·····

"Come now, and let us reason together,"
Says the LORD.
"Though your sins are like scarlet,
They shall be as white as snow;
Though they are red like crimson,
They shall be as wool.
If you are willing and obedient,
You shall eat the good of the land;
But if you refuse and rebel,
You shall be devoured by the sword."

Isaiah 1:18–20

Here we find the prophet Isaiah as he begins this lengthy book of prophecy spanning over forty years and four different kings of Judah. The prophet is having a conversation with God himself within the context of this book. The first thirty-nine chapters of Isaiah deal with the judgment of God upon Israel's spiritual infidelity. The last twenty-seven chapters deal with the themes of hope, promise, and the coming of Jesus Christ as the Savior of the world and the Messiah to the Jews. There are three observations I want to share that flow out of these verses.

The first observation is the word *communication*. When we think of communication, we think very simply about having an audible exchange or discourse. As human beings, we communicate with our families, friends, and co-workers. It is challenging to get along in this world without communication. Some people do not have the gift or ability to speak. Here we find communication not between two men, but between the prophet Isaiah and God Himself, the God who created Isaiah, the God who created all things, and who chose Israel as his visible community of faith in the Old Covenant. This exchange between God and Isaiah is striking in that God is the one initiating the communication. He is the one who is reaching out to Israel and a fallen humanity with an invitation, if you will, a beckoning for sinful man to flee to Himself and call upon His everlasting mercy.

Today, the Lord communicates to us through His inspired Word. We call it the Bible, and it consists of the Old and New Testaments. The Bible says that "all scripture is given by inspiration of God" (2 Timothy 3:16.) The Bible says that the prophets of old spoke not of private interpretation, but they spoke as "they were moved by the Holy Spirit" (2 Peter 1:21).

The Holy Spirit is the author of the Word of God, and so we receive communication from God today through His Word. His Spirit inspired this very text and every human writer included in the Bible. The same Spirit living in us in the twenty-first century as born again Christians and followers of Jesus Christ. Oh, to see the communication here! God says, "Come now, let us reason together." He is inviting exchange. He is condescending from His lofty throne of holiness and majesty, stooping down to our level of fallen humanity. He is saying, "Come now, and let us reason together. . . . Though your sins are like scarlet they shall be as white as snow" (Isaiah 1:18). So, we see communication between God and Isaiah.

Secondly is the word *eradication*. The word eradication means to kill or eliminate. This word depicts well this language about sins which are like scarlet becoming as white as snow. We see that God continues to communicate here the beauty of His free grace and mercy, which is encapsulated in the person and redemptive work of Jesus Christ. Later in the book of Isaiah, specifically Isaiah 53, we find the gospel according to Isaiah, as we call it today, with the prediction and prophecy and pronouncement of the coming of Christ in the fullness of time to this earth as the redeemer of sinful men. In graphic detail, Jesus Christ in His glory is communicated there, "All we like sheep have gone astray; We have turned, every one, to his own way; And the LORD has laid on Him the iniquity of us all" (Isaiah 53:6). Who is that? It is the Lord Jesus Christ. The Lord Jesus Christ is the redemptive thread, the redemptive person from Genesis 1 through Revelation 22. And so, the eradication of our sin is the removal of our sin. This does not happen by our good works or by our good intentions. It does not happen by our spiritual karma or some type of inner meditation and emptying out. It comes only through the gospel of Jesus Christ and the Holy Spirit of God applying the blood of Christ to sinners such as you and me.

Oh, dear friend in the marketplace, today there is a great need to declare this message of the free grace of Jesus Christ. Eradication of sin is something the old divines talked about in the 17th century. One was named John Owen, who wrote the book *The Death of Death*. It is of graphic detail on that exposition of Scripture with illustration and application about how Jesus Christ's death on the cross killed the penalty of sin. How, when He shed His blood, was in offering His blood and righteousness, and then the expiation of removing the sinfulness and enmity that God had toward us because of our sin. It is a glorious thing. Eradication means God through the blood. The imputed righteousness of Christ. We receive this through faith. He removes that sin which is dark red in this picture. We become white and clean as a picture of the riches of Jesus Christ. Oh, this is a glorious truth that the marketplace needs to hear today.

So many live in spiritual darkness. So many are busy making a living with no thought for the next life. So many prepare for only this world, neglecting preparation for the next world. Oh, dear friend, as Christ's church today—this is our day and time to take the gospel out into the marketplace and into the streets. More than ever, we must proclaim the eradication of sin because of Christ's redemptive work, available to all who believe in Him.

The last word or observation is the word *application*. God initiated this conversation with Isaiah just as He is the initiator in our salvation. What a wonderful message of hope with a personal application for our lives. God does not eradicate the sins of groups. He does not remove the sins and His enmity against crowds. It is one person at a time. The gospel of Jesus Christ is a personal gospel.

When Jesus died on the cross, dear friend, it was a real atonement. It was not a hypothetical atonement. He died for real sinners such as you and me. Aren't you thankful that Jesus Christ in all His glory, as He was lifted high on the cross and was exalted, is still drawing men and women to Himself? God has granted Jesus sinners from every tribe, tongue, and nation, and many are hearing the gospel in this generation who have yet to hear it. Many are receiving the Bible in their own dialect for the first time. Clearly, we see the good news of the gospel here, and the application is that we must go out and tell those who have never heard about Jesus Christ and how He saved sinners. We must go out and tell those who have not heard the full gospel that Jesus Christ is the savior of sinners and that He is the door of salvation. That door remains open to whosoever will, would come and respond to the message of the gospel.

Oh, Isaiah heard from God. Dear friend, have you heard from God? I am not asking if you have heard a plenary voice or whether you have heard God audibly. I am asking if your spirit deep in your soul has heard from God through His inspired Word? His Word is objective. His Word is never changing. It is the eternal Word of God. Today, there are those in the marketplace who trust in the subjective mystical whims of religion and even false gospels or cults that flow from Christian orthodoxy. Oh, that they would hear this good news. God has not said, "Go from me," but He has said, "Come let us reason together." Oh dear friend, let us take the good news of Jesus Christ and the salvation for sinners across the street and around the world.

God bless you, my friend.

DAY 7

· · + ◆ + · ·

There was a certain rich man who was clothed in purple and fine linen and fared sumptuously every day. But there was a certain beggar named Lazarus, full of sores, who was laid at his gate, desiring to be fed with the crumbs which fell from the rich man's table. Moreover the dogs came and licked his sores. So it was that the beggar died, and was carried by the angels to Abraham's bosom. The rich man also died and was buried. And being in torments in Hades, he lifted up his eyes and saw Abraham afar off, and Lazarus in his bosom.

Then he cried and said, "Father Abraham, have mercy on me, and send Lazarus that he may dip the tip of his finger in water and cool my tongue; for I am tormented in this flame." But Abraham said, "Son, remember that in your lifetime you received your good things, and likewise Lazarus evil things; but now he is comforted and you are tormented. And besides all this, between us and you there is a great gulf fixed, so that those who want to pass from here to you cannot, nor can those from there pass to us."

Luke 16:19–26

*H*ere we find the Lord Jesus talking about two people. There are parables all around this text in other chapters, but Jesus would always begin by saying this is a parable. It is interesting in this passage He does not say this is a parable, so we can assume there was indeed a rich man and a man named Lazarus. There are three words I want to share flowing out of this portion of Scripture.

The first word is *dichotomy*. Dichotomy means a contrast or a difference. Here we find two men, a rich man, and a poor man. When God looks into our hearts, he does not see us based on whether we are rich or poor, black or white. Whether we are of some social class or another. Every person is seen in terms of whether they have a saving relationship with God through Jesus Christ. Here Jesus was talking about a rich man who was blessed in life.

There is nothing sinful about being a rich man. The Bible says that God gives the power to create wealth (Deuteronomy 8:18), and if wealth is secured and businesses developed through proper methods with integrity within a capitalistic structure. All glory to God as long as that person has committed their life and all they have to God. On the other hand, there is nothing super spiritual for a person to be poor. Jesus said in Matthew 26:11 that the poor will be with us always. As Christ's people in the church, we should reach out to those who are in poverty. We should want to empower and enable them in a holistic way by equipping them in terms of being productive citizens in the kingdom of God. Being poor is not meritorious and being rich does not disqualify a person from being saved.

Jesus said it is very difficult for a rich man to be saved (Matthew 19:23). Today, there are many in the marketplace who are wealthy, business owners or corporate boards, CEOs, or entrepreneurs. They have much wealth, but this in no way disqualifies them from being born again by the gospel. Jesus said that "it is easier for a camel to go through the eye of a needle than for a rich man to [be saved]" (Matthew 19:24). Paul said to the Corinthians that "not many mighty, not many noble, are called" (1 Corinthians 1:26), but that means there are some. Praise the Lord! My prayer is that God, through His gospel, through you and I, as we go into the marketplace, would see those who are maybe with many possessions or no possessions, would come under conviction and be saved. There is a dichotomy between these two men, but that dichotomy is from a spiritual perspective. Is a person right with God?

The second observation is the word *demonstration*. The Bible teaches that we are saved by grace through faith and not by works, but it teaches how we live our lives and how the truths we believe are demonstrated. Or it shows there's evidence of that visibly, and those do bear witness to what our core belief is. This rich man lived for himself to build his own enterprise, and it was a comfort. Although you see he did some benevolent deeds—he did have his crumbs go out to the poor. That is what Lazarus ate. That was a good deed. However, there is no one good but God. Our goodness is His filthy rags from a human standpoint.

Then there was this poor man who had very little in life from an earthly standpoint, but, from heaven's perspective, he had that saving faith and trust in God, the gospel, and the Lord Jesus Christ. As soon as he died, he entered into the presence of God. Now, we see Jesus reference Abraham. This was because Abraham was viewed as the father of the Jewish faith. Jesus used that so it would be a familiar language to His listeners—Father Abraham. We find the poor man Lazarus, immediately going into glory with the Father when he died, The rich man, when he closed his eyes on earth, opened them to torment in hell. Even though works do not save us, a saving faith will give evidence and bear fruit. This rich man did not have faith in the Lord Jesus Christ and His gospel, which is why he went to hell. Oh, dear friend, we have an

God has placed you in a different place that contrasts with some other place where another believer is in your location. Your vocation is a place to demonstrate your faith in Jesus Christ.

opportunity with the dichotomies in the marketplace within our culture. God has placed you in a different place that contrasts with some other place where another believer is in your location. Your vocation is a place to demonstrate your faith in Jesus Christ. Though this poor man Lazarus lived his life with nothing on earth, he received the gift of eternal life and abundant life for all eternity because he was right with God through saving faith. And yet, the rich man went to hell where God's wrath is poured out on those who have died in unbelief. They are there where God's holiness is glorified and justified though God does not desire to see the death of the wicked.

The third word is *destination*. The poor man was in heaven with Jesus, and the rich man was in hell. There was a great gulf, a great separation between heaven and hell. Oh, did you catch the language today? Our Lord used very graphic vocabulary showing this dichotomy in this demonstration and even describing the destinations. Those in hell who died in unbelief because of their sin have memories. They are interactive. They have a sensibility that they rejected the good news of Jesus Christ in their earthly lives. The Bible says it is appointed on a man once to die and then the judgment (Hebrews 9:27).

Dear friend, there is no purgatory. There is no intermediary state for anyone. Once we give up our breath here, we go before God. That will be the day God will either welcome us into His paradise in Heaven, represented where Lazarus and Abraham are, or we will be in a place called hell. That place where God's wrath is upon those who have rejected the gospel of Jesus Christ.

There are those in the marketplace who need to hear the truth of the gospel. Many have never heard the authentic gospel, that we are saved by grace through faith in Jesus Christ alone. Not through religious rituals. It is not through observing sacraments and ordinances. It is not through being ceremonial and even depriving ourselves of things in this world or of being benevolent. It is only through the perfect righteousness of Jesus Christ in his vicarious atoning blood that is imputed to sinners like you and me, as we are declared righteous through faith in Christ. That is the good news of the gospel. Each day, may we demonstrate in our lives this saving faith that we have by loving God and His gospel with all our heart, mind, soul, and strength and then by loving our neighbors. This includes those outside of Christ, like the rich man who, though they are lost, still have hope because they have breath.

God bless you, my friend.

DAY 8

·••✦✦✦••·

But God, who is rich in mercy, because of His great love with which He loved us, even when we were dead in trespasses, made us alive together with Christ (by grace you have been saved), and raised us up together, and made us sit together in the heavenly places in Christ Jesus, that in the ages to come He might show the exceeding riches of His grace in His kindness toward us in Christ Jesus.

Ephesians 2:4–7

*H*ere we find a portion of scripture in Ephesians chapter two, which is that great explanation of our salvation in Jesus Christ. It is a rich salvation, a full of salvation, so free in salvation. I want to focus on two words that are like a pivot—literally a conjunction that we find at the beginning of verse 2—the phrase "but God." There are three observations I want to share about this one phrase within the context of Ephesians 2 and within its entirety.

First of all, *God did the impossible.* Before Ephesians 2:2, we read about the sinful nature of man. It is your sinful nature. It is my sinful nature. Everyone, born since Adam, was born as sinners by nature and by choice. Salvation is an impossibility from a human perspective, and God did the impossible. We cannot manufacture it. We cannot construct it. We cannot achieve it on our own. It must be God in his grace, working in and through us, through his glorious gospel of Jesus Christ. The Scripture says it is impossible for anyone in the flesh to be able to be born again without the gospel of Jesus Christ. Jeremiah 13:23 says, "Can the Ethiopian change his skin or the leopard its spots? Then may you also do good who are accustomed to do evil."

As we read in the book of Acts, Paul spent three years with the Ephesians. He had invested his life in Ephesus, and he had seen many come to faith in Christ through repentance and faith. He was writing this letter as a word of instruction and exhortation. It has doctrine. It has application. The apostle Paul clearly saw the fact that God did the impossible as he went into these unreached people groups on his missionary journey in Asia Minor (which is present-day Turkey). Paul saw God do the impossible. He saw "but God" with his own eyes, and you and I can see it today by faith.

Paul saw God do the impossible. He saw "but God" with his own eyes, and you and I can see it today by faith.

In the marketplace today, the same God of Ephesus is the God who rules and reigns in our generation. The same God of salvation who sent Paul to proclaim the gospel so the Ephesians could be saved is the same God searching out those in the marketplace today. "But God . . ." Those two words should ring in your ears. They should be an echo for all of your life that God did the impossible. What is impossible with man is possible with God through his work of grace in the gospel of Jesus Christ.

The second observation is that *God did the improbable.* Did you catch that? He did the improbable. Now, this is the great mystery of the ages. Why would a holy God in heaven, a God of justice and righteousness, and yes of wrath, be mindful of sinful men like you and me? Who are you? Psalm 8:4 says that God is mindful of men. That is the question today. *God, what prompted you to send your beloved Son so that we, as sinners, could be reconciled to our loving Creator?* That's right. It was improbable. "But God . . ."

Oh, do you see the beauty in those two words? I remember years ago when I heard a message by the late Dr. Martin Lloyd Jones. I listened to many of his sermons on audio and read many of his books. Many called him a prince, a preacher in London in Westminster Chapel when he ministered in the twentieth century. I remember hearing a message he preached on these two words, and God used that message to prick my heart and to show me these truths that He not only did the impossible, but He also did the improbable. Charles Wesley wrote that great hymn "And Can It Be That I Should Gain." The words are striking from Scripture, but one phrase strikes me today. "How can it be that thou, my God, shouldst die for me?" It is improbable. It is impossible.

The third observation is that *God did the indescribable.* "But God . . ." This can be illustrated almost like going through a revolving door into a shopping center or an office building. In the hustle and bustle of urban America, you suddenly see a door change direction. The apostle Paul used a conjunction phrase in a strategic point because he was pivoting from the depravity of man and the spiritual deadness of man. Man is helpless unless God intervenes and rescues him through His gospel. Here's the pivot. "But God." The verse that we read, and those after it in Ephesians, continue to declare and describe the grace of God in Jesus Christ. I tell you, dear friend, there are those in the marketplace today who have never heard this gospel of grace. I am not saying that they have never been to a church. I am not saying they have never heard a message in a sanctuary, nor am I saying they have not read the Bible. I am saying that many have not heard the gospel of Jesus

Christ in the sense that they have received the truth of the gospel and had it invade their minds in their hearts and wills.

Oh, friend, the Holy Spirit of God is at work today. Just as He roamed above the waters at creation in Genesis chapter 1, so the Spirit of God is roaming among the marketplace. He is searching out hearts. He is testifying that Jesus Christ is Lord and Savior. He is using mouthpieces like you and me. Yes, "but God," He did the indescribable. It is hard to have a vocabulary that can adequately describe these truths of the gospel of grace. As Paul described this to the Corinthians, *it is an unspeakable gift,* which is the Lord Jesus Christ, and God is giving His beloved Son for sinners such as you and me, so we could be redeemed. There is no dictionary of man that contains the words needed to describe the glory of the gospel effectively.

Dear friend, here is the good news. The door of salvation is still open. Those in the boardroom and community center need to hear that Jesus Christ saved to the uttermost. You and I have the privilege and opportunity to take the gospel across the street and around the world. We can persuade those outside of Christ to repent, turn to Him, and receive this glorious gift of salvation.

God bless you, my friend.

DAY 9

····◆◆◆····

Then Samson called to the Lord, saying, "O Lord God, remember me, I pray! Strengthen me, I pray, just this once, O God, that I may with one blow take vengeance on the Philistines for my two eyes!" And Samson took hold of the two middle pillars which supported the temple, and he braced himself against them, one on his right and the other on his left. Then Samson said, "Let me die with the Philistines!" And he pushed with all his might, and the temple fell on the lords and all the people who were in it. So the dead that he killed at his death were more than he had killed in his life.

Judges 16:28–30

*H*ere we find a man named Samson who lived during the time of the judges. As a matter of fact, he was a judge of Israel. We see several different individuals, men and women, such as Gideon and Deborah, and here we find another one. Samson was raised up by God to be a deliverer of His people from the enemy. The enemy of Israel during this time was a nation called the Philistines. They were a pagan group. They were God-haters, and their whole purpose was to extinguish the work of God by harming the Israelites and taking them into captivity. Here are three observations I want to share flowing out of these verses.

First, let us look at *how Samson started*. He was born to a couple who had been barren for many years. His father's name was Manoah. We do not know his mother's name, but they had prayed for a child, and one day God blessed them with a son they named Samson.

From his birth, Samson was to be consecrated to the Lord. At that time, there was something called a Nazarite vow found in the Old Testament law. A child, consecrated or set apart, lived their lives in a special way, under certain regulations. There were three major requirements under the Nazarite vow. The Nazarite could not cut his hair because it was a sign or symbol of God's anointing upon them in their hair follicles. They could not consume any alcohol, nor could they have any contact with a corpse.

His parents committed Samson with this vow which came from God. That is how his life began and how he grew up.

We find this in the narrative beginning in Judges chapter 13 and what we just read in chapter 16. Samson was anointed by the Spirit of God. He was given great strength, and we find he started with a consecrated life committed by his parents, anointed by God, and in obedience.

Dear friend, as we look at our culture, a lot is changing in our world, even in areas with a strong gospel influence or a vibrant community of faith within Christendom. We see how the world, the flesh, and the devil began to come in, and society as an Antichrist culture begins to try and extinguish the Christian witness. It was no different in Samson's time than in our time. Let us beware and note that there is an enemy who seeks to take us down. It may not be a visible people group like the Philistines in an earthly battle. Today it is spiritual warfare. It is the prince of darkness of the air

Today it is spiritual warfare. It is the prince of darkness of the air who seeks to advance the kingdom of darkness, and so there is a conflict between the light and the darkness.

who seeks to advance the kingdom of darkness, and so there is a conflict between the light and the darkness.

The second observation about Samson's life is not only how he started but then *how he lived*. Samson was a human being just like you and me. He had temptations that came his way. Samson had times of testing from God, and as he advanced the kingdom of God in his space, he had weaknesses in his flesh. He was enticed or tempted by pagan women who were part of the Philistines, and he struggled with this. There may be some of you who struggle with these types of temptations. Samson was no different than we are in our culture today. There is a lust of the eyes, the lust of the flesh, and the pride of life. Samson unfortunately, made some bad decisions. He made some choices that were not in accordance with God's will or in accordance with His word, and so Samson ran into serious roadblocks in his advance of the kingdom in his space.

One of those was when he met Delilah. Delilah was a Philistine woman with whom Samson had a relationship. She began to ask Samson how he had his strength. Samson was a riddler, if you will. He liked to play jokes, and he would not tell the truth. One day he told her his strength came from his hair. That was a secret of his strength. Delilah was in a conspiracy with the Philistines to capture Samson, and that was all she wrote, folks. Samson's hair was cut. He woke up, and the Bible says that the power of God had departed from him. It looked like Samson's ministry was over. It looked like his sphere of influence as a judge within Israel and a kingdom leader ended. He had gone from Alpha to Omega, the beginning to the end. He would be a footnote in the history of how those who have fallen prey to the world or the enemy within a culture, as a man of faith who failed.

The third observation shows how God is a *God of grace, and how God is a God of restoration*, even when it looks like it's all over from the world's perspective. Here's a third observation. *How Samson finished.*

The verses we read today talk about how he finished. He desired to leave this life glorifying God by defeating the Philistines. You see, that was his calling. It may sound grotesque or brutal to us today, but at this time in the Old Covenant, the people of Israel were God's anointed people, chosen to be His light to a dark world. Gentiles would attack them, and in this instance, that nation was the Philistines. Samson's role was to deliver Israel from the Philistines. He was fulfilling his calling.

The Philistines poked his eyes out. They held him in chains. Three thousand people came together at the theater to see Samson. He was like a freak show. It would be like a circus today where they would flaunt men who served the God of the Bible, the God of Israel. They had captured him, wounded him, and taken away his strength and his power. Now they would make a mockery of God and God's servant.

Samson cried out to the Lord for strength. He prayed for another anointing or an infusion of strength from God. In these last moments, Samson pushed the pillars. The Bible says there were three thousand Philistines who went to their death. In Samson's death, he killed more Philistines than he did in his life. Samson was a man who finished strong in the sense that even when he had fallen and was yet without strength, he was restored to glorify God. Samson had many faults. He had many weaknesses, just like you and me. Samson's message today is that it is never too late to come to repentance, forsake your sin, and surrender yourself to God's will for your life. It is never too late. It does not matter if you are a child, a teenager, a young adult, or a middle-aged or older adult. God is a restoring God, and He wants to use us as we surrender to Him.

You see, in Hebrews 11, Samson was listed in the hall of faith. Yes, there's just a little sentence about him. He does not have a paragraph like some of the other patriarchs, but there is a sentence that said "of whom the world was not worthy" (Hebrews 11:38). Samson is included in that list, and as a man who God called from birth, who stumbled during his journey of faith, but who then, by God's grace, was restored to a point where he could end his life glorifying God with the defeat of the enemy.

May you and I today seek the Lord and know that God is restoring us regardless of our past, where we have been, or how we failed. In the marketplace today, there are those who need to hear this message that God has not given up on us and that He is a God of grace.

Let us share that message, share that truth, the good news, the gospel, and herald it all around the marketplace across the street— and around the world. God bless you, my friend.

DAY 10

· · · ✦ ✦ ✦ ✦ · ·

In the year that King Uzziah died, I saw the Lord sitting on a throne, high and lifted up, and the train of His robe filled the temple. Above it stood Seraphim; each one had six wings: with two he covered his face, with two he covered his feet, and with two he flew. And one cried to another and said:

"Holy, holy, holy is the LORD of hosts;
the whole earth is full of His glory!"

And the posts of the door were shaken by the voice of him who cried out, and the house was filled with smoke.

So I said:
"Woe is me, for I am undone!
Because I am a man of unclean lips,
And I dwell in the midst of a people of unclean lips;
For my eyes have seen the King,
the LORD of hosts."

Then one of the seraphim flew to me, having in his hand a live coal which he had taken with the tongs from the altar. And he touched my mouth with it, and said:

"Behold, this has touched your lips;
Your iniquity is taken away,
And your sin purged."

Also I heard the voice of the Lord, saying

"Whom shall I send,
And who will go for Us?"

Then I said, "Here am I! Send me."

Isaiah 6:1–9

*O*h, what an incredible passage! During the Old Testament times, a king named Uzziah reigned over the people of God in Judah as king for fifty-two years. And when he died, it was a very dark day in Judah. Everyone asked, "How can we go forward and proceed under the direction of God?" And there was a prophet named Isaiah who was looking for truth. And Isaiah was close to God.

There are three observations I want to share from this text.

First, Isaiah had a *glimpse of the deity*. Did you notice it says, "In the year that King Uzziah died, I saw the Lord sitting on a throne, high and lifted up, and the train of his robe filled the temple"? Come close for just a minute and think about that. Even as the Word of God reveals His majesty, this was the God of Israel. Hear me today. This is the same God you and I can know today in a personal relationship through Jesus Christ. With all these angels flying around the throne and singing, "Holy, holy, holy . . . the whole earth is full of His glory!" This is the deity of God.

> **There are many false gods. Many gods are created in man's image to serve humanity's purpose, but there is only one true God, and He is the God of the Bible. He is the God of the nations.**

There are many false gods. Many gods are created in man's image to serve humanity's purpose, but there is only one true God, and He is the God of the Bible. He is the God of the nations. He is the God of those being called to Christ, to the gospel, from every tribe, tongue, and kindred. It is the deity of God. It is a glimpse that Isaiah had that you and I can have by faith.

Today we must understand the gospel to be God-centered. Are you listening? Many in the marketplace and even within the sanctuaries and worship centers proclaim a half-full gospel. It is half empty. This is not the true gospel of Jesus Christ. Dear friend, we must see the deity of God, the Triune God, as revealed in Scripture before we can ever have a proper biblical worldview. It is God the Father, God the Son, God the Spirit—the Trinity as we call it. This is the one and only deity who has created us and bought mankind through the redemption of Jesus Christ.

The second observation is a *glimpse of depravity*. Do you notice as Isaiah first sees God, then and only then, is he able to see the condition of man? If you do not have a proper view of God according to Scripture, if you have too low a view of God, and you bring Him down to humanity's level, you will not see the deity of God lifted high on His throne. Only when we glimpse God's deity, can we see our sinfulness and depravity. Depravity means that we are all born sinners by nature. We have inherited Adam's sin and guilt, and one day we will become sinners by choice whenever we come to the age where we can make those choices of moral transgression. We come into this world as guilty sinners, and we need the grace of God.

We cannot see our depravity unless we first see His deity and holiness. God is holy, and we are not. God is God. You and I are not. We must see our sinfulness and understand we are sinners in need of a savior. Someone said in years past that you and I are great sinners, but we all have a great Savior, Jesus Christ. The depravity of man—you and I have it. It is an infection. It is a disease. It pollutes us, and because of our depravity, we cannot ascend to the holiness of God, except through the righteousness of Jesus Christ. We receive this through repentance and faith.

Oh, the marketplace needs to hear that man is not getting better. This world is not improving from a spiritual perspective. This world is under the curse. The world, the flesh, and the devil seek to take down those who are the redeemed of the Lord. They want to stop the advance of the kingdom of God. Oh, dear friend, today what a word, a challenge from Isaiah that we see our depravity. "Woe is me, for I am undone! Because I am a man of unclean lips."

Oh, would you confess with me your own sinfulness? I confess my sinfulness before God. I see that I am not what I should be but thank God I am not what I will be by His grace as the gospel transforms me, as I live for Jesus Christ, and as Jesus Christ lives in and through me.

Our third observation is that Isaiah had a *glimpse of duty*. Isaiah then had the altar throngs touched to his lips—the cleansing. This is a picture of the purging of his sin, symbolizing how the blood of Jesus in the New Covenant takes away our sin. There is that purging. What happened after he had a glimpse of deity and a glimpse of depravity? He had a glimpse of duty. Whenever we see God for who He is as revealed in the Scripture, whenever we see ourselves as the Scripture declares us to be—we know by our experience as sinners, who needs the grace of God and forgiveness of God, then we will see our duty. The normal response for a person who is born again by the gospel, one who comes to repentance and faith in Christ his Lord, is to ask, *What would you have me to do? Where would you have me to go? Here am I! Send me.* Isaiah did not say, "Here I am. Send me." Me, like I am staying here. He said, *here am I.* It was mobility.

Isaiah said, *I will go, God, wherever you call me to go. Wherever you lead, I will follow.* Is that your prayer today? Is that your prayer?

That God will use you to advance the kingdom in the market-place, office, board rooms, parks, theatres, and stadiums? Oh, dear friend, maybe God is calling you to go around the world on a mission trip. Praise God, be obedient, and go. Be different. Maybe God is calling you to go across the street in your community and proclaim the everlasting gospel. There are those in the market-place, in our society, who need to hear the gospel of Jesus Christ, the unadulterated simple and pure gospel of Jesus Christ, and His love for sinners. Would you join me in taking this gospel across the street and around the world? What a wonderful duty.

God bless you, my friend.

DAY 11

· · · ✦ ✦ ✦ ✦ · · ·

Then Jesus entered and passed through Jericho. Now behold, there was a man named Zacchaeus who was a chief tax collector, and he was rich. And he sought to see who Jesus was, but could not because of the crowd, for he was of short stature. So he ran ahead and climbed up into a sycamore tree to see Him, for He was going to pass that way. And when Jesus came to the place, He looked up and saw him, and said to him, "Zacchaeus, make haste and come down, for today I must stay at your house." So he made haste and came down, and received Him joyfully. But when they saw it, they all complained, saying, "He has gone to be a guest with a man who is a sinner."

Then Zacchaeus stood and said to the Lord, "Look, Lord, I give half of my goods to the poor; and if I have taken anything from anyone by false accusation, I restore fourfold."

And Jesus said to him, "Today salvation has come to this house, because he also is a son of Abraham; for the Son of Man has come to seek and to save that which was lost."

Luke 19:1–10

*H*ere we see in the context that the Lord Jesus is on His way to Jerusalem for His Passion week. He would become the Lamb of God who would give His life for the sins of the world. He passed through this city called Jericho. The history of Jericho in the Old Testament, if you remember, was when Joshua and his army brought the walls down by a miracle of God. When Jericho was defeated, God said the city was not to be rebuilt, for it was a cursed city. Here we are, many years later, and the city is rebuilt by a new generation living during Jesus' time. Jesus chose to go through Jericho on the way to Jerusalem. Three observations come from this passage.

Notice *the path of the Lord*. This was a specific path. It was a path He did not have to take. Jesus was intentional in His earthly ministry, and He knew exactly where He was going to go and what He was going to do. So, it is interesting that Jesus came to this city called Jericho, a city cursed by the Old Testament law. Jesus Christ came into this world to redeem those under the law because of the curse, as He was to be made a curse for us when He would go to Jerusalem. Here, we see Jesus leading by example, and in His path, there was a divine appointment. On the path of the Lord, there was a man named Zacchaeus, in Jericho, who needed to be saved. It continues today in our generation. Jesus Christ uses us as His mouthpiece, as His prophets, if you will. It is not our message. It is His message, and the same message that was on this path through Jericho, for this one man, Zacchaeus, is the message we have today. It is the power of God unto salvation. That's what the gospel is to all, unto each, who believe in Jesus Christ.

> **Jesus Christ uses us as His mouthpiece, as His prophets, if you will. It is not our message. It is His message.**

The second observation I want you to consider is *the presence of the Lord*. He came into this city, and there was a large crowd.

Scripture says there were many people there, and apparently, Zacchaeus was a short man. He could not see Jesus. Scripture also tells us that his vocation was a tax collector. He worked for the Roman Gentile government, yet he was from one of the twelve tribes of Israel. This was a Jewish man who worked for the pagan government, and his responsibility was to collect the taxes from the constituents of this region, which included other sons of Abraham in the flesh. Zacchaeus was seen as a traitor. He was a chief tax collector who happened to be rich. Most in that vocation were rich as they were compensated for their collections. Maybe he even worked on commission, so the people despised him.

When he saw Christ enter into Jericho, the Bible says Zacchaeus, who was short in stature, wanted to be elevated to a posture where he could see Jesus for himself. The presence of the Lord was apparent to the whole crowd as Christ walked through the marketplace. But there was one specific man who Jesus had his eyes on. It was this man Zacchaeus. Zacchaeus was in the sycamore tree, and Jesus confronted him. Jesus placed his eyes on him and said, "Come down, for today I must stay at your house." What an encouragement today that the presence of the Lord Jesus Christ was not with the elite, not with the institutional religious people.

His presence was in the marketplace. His presence was with those who were cast out of the community of the faith of Judaism. His presence was with those who needed salvation, those who realized the need. Jesus said that He did not come as the great physician to heal the righteous, but He came to heal the sick. Dear friend, before a person can be saved, he must come to repentance and faith in Jesus Christ, and that means there is an acknowledgment and an affirmation that he is a sinner. We all fall short of the glory of God, and we need the personal presence of Christ.

Dear friend, like Zacchaeus, we have the Word of God. We have the Holy Spirit of God, who is everywhere and can work with any person in terms of the redemptive work of grace that God does through His gospel penetrating the hearts of sinners. The presence of our Lord here was within the crowd, but it was specifically focused on this one man, Zacchaeus.

The third observation is *the pardon of the Lord*. When Zacchaeus came down, the Bible said that he immediately gave forth fruit of repentance in terms of his intentions. He told the Lord that anything he had stolen would be returned. In fact, he would give fourfold restitution to those he had taken something from by a false account. The Bible says when we are born again through Jesus Christ, we are new creatures. Old things are passed away. Behold, all things become new. This man named Zacchaeus became a friend of God as he was reconciled through faith in the Lord Jesus Christ. Jesus said to him, "today salvation has come to this house." Jesus was going to Calvary days after this, but Zacchaeus had the eyes of faith to see that this Jesus who was before him was not just a man. He was and is the God-man. He saw Jesus had come to seek and to save his life. The pardon of the Lord is when God, who is holy, looks down on us who are criminals because we are violators of God's law. We have rejected His love. Dear friend, we deserve to be in hell today, but God, in His mercy, came to us. God came to Zacchaeus. "For God so loved the world that He gave His only begotten Son, that whoever believes in Him should not perish but have everlasting life" (John 3:16).

Oh, how great is the pardon of our Lord granted, by the judge Himself, Jesus Christ, received by the criminal! Oh, that was a great day in Jericho! It was a picture of grace. Jesus Christ receives sinners. Have you received him today?

God bless you, my friend.

DAY 12

···+◆+···

Masters, give your bondservants what is just and fair, knowing that you also have a Master in heaven.

Continue earnestly in prayer, being vigilant in it with thanksgiving; meanwhile praying also for us, that God would open to us a door for the word, to speak the mystery of Christ, for which I am also in chains, that I may make it manifest, as I ought to speak.

Walk in wisdom toward those who are outside, redeeming the time. Let your speech always be with grace, seasoned with salt, that you may know how you ought to answer each one.

Colossians 4:1–6

These words in the book of Colossians, written by the apostle Paul, are inspired by the Holy Spirit. He was writing this letter to the church at Colossae, which was a church in Asia Minor. He was writing to declare some doctrinal truths regarding the supremacy of Christ in all things and that Christ was head of the church. Within this letter, we find three striking words coming from a man who was actually in prison when he was writing this epistle.

There is the word *conversation*. Do you notice that Paul asked the Colossians to pray for him and those with him, that God would open a door for the Word to speak? The Bible talks a lot about doors. God says that when He closes a door, no man can open it, but when He opens a door, no man can close it (Isaiah 22:22). So here we have the apostle Paul who is constrained physically yet is asking for prayer that he might be able to go forth as a witness for Jesus Christ within his space of influence. There must be a conversation to communicate the gospel. Friend, in the marketplace today, many conversations deal with a vast number of subject matters. Some deal with commercial enterprises or with philosophical ideas. Others center around social and civic affairs but hear me today. There is a scarcity of conversations focused on the person and work of Jesus Christ. There might be religious conversations. Paul was not talking about having a door open to share religious truths, attributes, or even principles. He wanted God to open a door for him to go forth and have gospel conversations. A gospel conversation is simply a conversation centered around Jesus Christ.

No doubt, Paul was a great preacher of the gospel. Throughout the book of Acts, we see him preaching the gospel during his missionary journeys and in the synagogues, on the streets, and in the stadiums. The apostle Paul was very gifted in that anointing of biblical proclamation, but he was also focused on personal conversations with individuals and groups. The conversations he and Lydia shared, and several other conversations recorded in the book of Acts show us that he was focused on the door of entrance that God would open. He was able to have these conversations

The apostle Paul was very gifted in that anointing of biblical proclamation, but he was also focused on personal conversations with individuals and groups.

in different environments. He was always ready to present the mystery of Christ and the truth of the gospel.

The second word from this passage is *consideration*. When we talk about sharing the gospel, and as Paul was praying that he would have a door for the word to speak the mystery of Christ, we are primarily focused upon the claims of Jesus Christ. Paul understood that the claims of Christ were not limited only to his generation but that they were for all generations until Jesus Christ returns to this earth. The mystery of Christ here, which is Him speaking the Word of God, entails the essentials of the gospel in Christ's virgin birth, His virtuous life, His vicarious atoning death on the cross, His victorious body resurrection, and, yes dear friend, yet to come, His visible return to this earth from heaven. Paul was praying that the subject of his conversations would be Christ. Christ should always be the subject of a gospel conversation. Paul focused on having those opportunities to share Christ. Dear friend, this does not happen by accident. We must be intentional in our lives, as we are in the workplace and activities outside the church walls. This must be ingrained in our minds and embedded in our hearts, that those we meet are facing eternity, and the claims of Jesus Christ and how they respond to them will make the difference between where they spend eternity, whether in heaven or hell. There must be a sense of urgency here when we consider these truths.

Finally, the last word is *exhortation*. When we pray for an open door for the gospel, we must move toward the goal of calling someone to repentance and faith in Jesus Christ. The gospel is unique because it is a personal relationship between our Holy God in heaven and us as sinners on earth. That great gulf of separation, because of our sin, has created a situation where we must pray urgently for open doors, but we must also walk through those doors in terms of exhorting and calling men, women, and children to personal repentance of sin and faith in Jesus Christ.

Paul gave invitations to those he spoke with in the crowds and in conversations both mass evangelism and personal evangelism. His invitation, friend, was not an invitation to join a church. It was not an invitation to embark on a new religion. It was not an invitation to have a makeover or rehabilitation of one's own sinful life but, it was for individuals to be born again by the gospel of Jesus Christ.

Exhortation means we are encouraging, exhorting, and persuading with passion for God and for compassion for those we meet who need Christ in the marketplace. We are calling for the verdict. The question is the same for those who heard the gospel in Paul's time and those who will hear it now—What will you do with Jesus Christ? My prayer, dear friend, is that God would use you and I, and anyone who calls on the name of Christ, to pray for these open doors of opportunity to share Him, and to speak forth the words of life into others.

God bless you, my friend.

DAY 13

⋯⁺⁺◆⁺⁺⋯

*And Elijah came to all the people, and said, "How long will you falter between two opinions? If the L*ORD* is God, follow Him; but if Baal, follow him." But the people answered him not a word. Then Elijah said to the people, "I alone am left a prophet of the L*ORD*; but Baal's prophets are four hundred and fifty men. Therefore let them give us two bulls; and let them choose one bull for themselves, cut it in pieces, and lay it on the wood, but put no fire under it; and I will prepare the other bull, and lay it on the wood, but put no fire under it. Then you call on the name of your gods, and I will call on the name of the L*ORD*; and the God who answers by fire, He is God."*

So all the people answered and said, "It is well spoken."

1 Kings 18:21–24

Today we see the prophet Elijah, an Old Testament saint and a leader in God's kingdom. He was a prophet in Israel facing wicked opposition. King Ahab and Jezebel were reigning on the throne. The day came when the irritation of the world, the flesh, and the devil became so strong that it brought a confrontation with Elijah. There are three words I want to share with you from this passage.

The first was there was a *conflict*. Now Elijah was very aware of the opposition. The idolatry and the rebellion against the God of Israel had become rampant. God was, in a temporal way, judging the people. He was giving them over to their desires, and Elijah was one man who was in the marketplace of his time. He was there on Mount Carmel. I have been to Mount Carmel, where a statue is erected looking out over the valley, we call Megiddo Valley. I have seen the landscape in this century, but Elijah was there many years before Christ. On that day, as Elijah stood there, many were in opposition, and he was the minority. There was a conflict. Elijah told the people they must decide who they would serve. They could not serve the God of the Bible and Baal. He drew a line in the sand. Today there may be occasions or circumstances where you, dear friend, are challenged for your faith in Jesus Christ. You are opposed and may even be persecuted because you name the name of Christ. This conflict is something that God is giving you that you might have an opportunity to proclaim His excellencies and be conduits of the glory of God manifesting in the darkness and the idolatry of this world.

There on Mount Carmel, the conflict took place. There were four hundred fifty prophets of Baal versus one man. I am not a betting man, but I know if Las Vegas rated the odds on Elijah, he would not have much of a chance. But you know, one person plus God is a majority, and we know the majority of people in this world, as in the crowd with Elijah, were all on that broad road to destruction that leads to death. You know, if

If you are on the narrow road and following Jesus Christ, it does not matter what the world, the opposition, enemy forces, or powers of darkness try to do to you. God is with you.

you are on the narrow road and following Jesus Christ, it does not matter what the world, the opposition, enemy forces, or powers of darkness try to do to you. God is with you. He will never leave you. You can be a person of influence even in the darkest places within your marketplace.

Secondly, notice there was a *contest* where Elijah, anointed by God as a prophet, wanted to facilitate the manifestation of God's glory in the midst of all of that pagan idolatry. He challenged the four hundred fifty prophets of Baal. Elijah challenged the prophets to bring two bulls, one for themselves and one for Elijah, to see whether Baal or the God of the Bible would send fire to burn the animal on the altar. The text reads that the pagan prophets called upon their false god Baal, and of course, it was silent. Then it was Elijah's turn. Notice before Elijah began speaking with men, he spoke with God first. He asked God to manifest His glory, show His strong omnipotent arm, and bring fire down from heaven to consume that bull and the wood. He was so confident that the God of the Bible would give him the victory for the glory of God that he even poured water upon the wood in the bowl. Water is the one thing that can put out the fire of man. But this was not the fire of man that came, dear friend. It was the fire of God. God rained down fire, consuming the bull and the sacrifice. There was a great victory for the God of the Bible and the man of God, Elijah.

When we have contests many times daily, there are challenges and temptations. The world, the flesh, and the devil want to tempt and distract you from being a person of influence in the marketplace for Christ. I want you to know that greater is He that is in you than in the world. I want you to know that God is with you every day when you face contests or encounters with the opposition. I pray He will be your shield and strength as you take the gospel to those who need to hear in their places of influence.

The last word is *conquest*. There was a conquest. There was a victory here. I mentioned the fire came down, and God was glorified in all of the people. It seemed they began to believe. When people see a miracle or some great manifestation, they often flock to the things of God, but only God knows who is truly born again by the gospel. God knows who has a real personal encounter, a conquest with the gospel, conquering sinful man and transforming their soul.

That has happened to me and my life. Has it happened to you? If so, we can be like Elijah and go forth, knowing that God provides victory for us through Jesus Christ.

Thank you, dear friend.

DAY 14

····◆◆◆····

Ho! Everyone who thirsts,
Come to the waters;
And you who have no money,
Come, buy and eat.
Yes, come, buy wine and milk
Without money and without price.

Isaiah 55:1

ere we find the prophet Isaiah, six hundred plus years before
the coming of Christ. In this interlude within his sixty-six
chapters in the English Bible, we find the declaration, really the
exaltation of the free grace of God in Jesus Christ. Let us look at
the three observations that come from this verse.

The first observation is *the pronouncement*. Notice Isaiah
says, "Ho! Everyone who thirsts, come to the waters." Here
we find the King of the universe, the great God of heaven,
offering an invitation and calling those in the marketplace. This
pronouncement is the same for every generation. Isaiah is saying
for everyone—anyone that thirsts to come to God and seek forth
His mercy. Come to the waters. Many times, we think about

deities or authorities from a human perspective. We believe this higher power is peering down upon creation, looking to harm those who are not living in exact accordance with whatever its design or blueprint should be. Dear friend, the pronouncement from the God of the Bible through the prophet Isaiah, is that anyone and everyone can come to Him and drink of the living water. It will quench the thirst of a soul for all eternity—if only they would come and respond in repentance and faith to the gospel of Jesus Christ. Yes, this is the book of Isaiah, and it is on that side of the cross.

Let me remind you the Old Testament is simply the New Testament concealed, and the New Testament is merely the Old Testament revealed. There are types and pictures, portraits of the grace of God in the redemptive work of the Lord Jesus Christ all through the Old Testament and throughout the book of Isaiah. Here we see this pronouncement. It is an invitation from heaven to earth, saying anyone and everyone who thirsts may come to the living water of Jesus Christ.

Today there is a great drought and famine in the marketplace. Many in the marketplace are pursuing only commercial enterprise, trying to build a kingdom for themselves on earth, and accumulating all they can. Psalm 14:1 tells us that it is the fool who says in his heart there is no God. "For what will it profit a man if he gains the whole world, and loses his own soul?" (Mark 8:36). Dear friend, our life on earth is one where God intends for us to be in fellowship with Him through the Lord Jesus Christ, and we are living this life in preparation for the extended life of eternity. Isaiah mentions water that is not

Our life on earth is one where God intends for us to be in fellowship with Him through the Lord Jesus Christ, and we are living this life in preparation for the extended life of eternity.

primarily for the body or the physical thirst, but water for the soul. He is talking about the water that comes through Jesus Christ.

The second observation that flows from this verse is the pronouncement from God in heaven and *the prerequisite*. Notice Isaiah says, come those who have no money; come without price. This is contrary to the way the human economy will work in our commercial endeavors in the marketplace. Their exchanges are transactions that require consideration from both sides. In other words, the economies of past civilizations had the bartering system where services were exchanged for other services. The currency and coins then came into being. We find that even now in the twenty-first-century economy, transactions are done in the marketplace through adequate monetization and currency exchange because there is a value placed on a good or service. Dear friend, God's economy of redemption is different. He is the one who has paid the redemption price. The prerequisite is that we come to him, not with our payment through works and deeds or through our self-righteousness. There is nothing a sinner can bring to the table before a Holy God. There is no negotiation. There is no treaty. The sinner must come without anything in his hands. With empty hands, we bring to the cross of Christ, and we must cling to the Christ of the cross.

That is what Isaiah is pointing to here. He is declaring this pronouncement that the prerequisite for a sinner receiving the water of life is that he must come with a thirst for the righteousness of God and the shed blood of Jesus Christ as payment for his sin. That message is the everlasting gospel that continues from generation to generation, and how those we work and live with need to hear of the love of Jesus Christ. This is free grace. God extends this to sinners, and the prerequisite is that sinners know that they have no hope outside of the free grace of Christ.

A third observation is *the payment*. Notice I mentioned it earlier from the verse, without money and without price. In other words, we are to come and eat soul food, soul-nourishing food. We are to come and to understand the gift of God is His grace and that He has paid the redemption price in full for us. It is finished. It means it is done, payment in full. There is no more obligation for the sinner. He is no longer under the wrath of God if he will come under the blood of Jesus Christ and accept through faith the grace of God. It is implied in the text that we must reach out to God as He has first reached out to us. The grace of God has appeared to all men under salvation. The Scripture says God does not desire that anyone perish (2 Peter 3:9). God does not delight in the death of the wicked.

Oh, dear friend, would you join me today as a believer in Christ and as we go in the marketplace. Would you and I, would we together, filled with the Holy Spirit, be the mouth of Christ? So many need to hear there is water for the soul, from the living water, Jesus Christ. And there is no human payment of any kind, of merit, of penance, of outward ceremony, of even self-evaluation or positive thinking. None of that can make the payment. Only Jesus Christ has provided the payment satisfactory to a Holy God so sinners can drink of Christ, the living water. By faith, they can be reconciled and have eternal life with God. Is this your status today? Are you a born again believer in Christ? Join me as we work and share like it all depends on us in spreading this good news of the gospel but trusting that it is the work of the Holy Spirit. It is the Spirit of God that convicts of sin, righteousness, and judgment. The Spirit of God is always testifying to the truth of Jesus Christ. The Spirit of God always elevates Christ. Today, you and I must elevate Christ in the marketplace and know that this is the remedy for man's sin. Those who have nothing are qualified to come to Christ. Those who realize that they have no merit deserve the wrath of God, yet they repent of their sins and call on Christ can.

God bless you, my friend.

DAY 15

· · ◆ ◆ ◆ ◆ · ·

And when they had come to the place called Calvary, there they crucified Him, and the criminals, one on the right hand and the other on the left.

Luke 23:33

Here we find in this verse a historic day in the history of mankind. Jesus Christ, the Son of God, was taken by the Romans and was put on a cross. His execution was a form of capital punishment under the statutes of Caesar at that time. There are three observations I want to share with you.

First, we see *the place*. The Bible says there was a place called Calvary. This was an actual location, according to historians, outside of the old Jerusalem walls. The book of Hebrews says that this was outside the camp. It was a place of execution where criminals were killed for certain crimes committed against Rome. No doubt many had gone before Jesus and died on the cross at Calvary. Many historians called Calvary the skull because when looking up at the hill, it looked like the shape of a skull. Others have said it was called the skull because there were bones on the hillside. Regardless of what this place of execution was called, it was a literal place on earth that God created. God had ordained that this place would be where Jesus Christ, His beloved Son, would die for the sins of the world.

If you go to Jerusalem today, you will not be able to find the exact location of this place, for civilizations have come and gone. However, excavation uncovered remains that have pointed to specific locations within the current day Jerusalem. But here is the truth for us. Dear friend, though we may never stand in the exact place where Jesus died on the cross, we can know today that Jesus actually died at this place, and His death marked a pivot in human history. All of human history now centers on the cross and death of Jesus Christ.

The second observation is the word, *people*. Notice the Scripture says, "When they had come to the place called Calvary, there they . . ." I want to focus on the word *they* for a moment. There were many types of people who were around the cross. Remember, this was a place of execution, which occurred regularly. Criminals of Rome were put on public display, lifted up on a cross, and crucified with this agonizing death with many hours of pain and suffering amongst the ridicule of spectators watching from below. There were many kinds of men and women present that day at Calvary. There were Romans, and there were Jews—the holy and the hellish. There were children, and there were adults. It was as if, in this crowd, the eyes of the world were looking at Jesus Christ as He was lifted up and dying a criminal's death.

The Bible says Jesus Christ is the Lamb of God who came to take away the sins of the world.

The Bible says Jesus Christ is the Lamb of God who came to take away the sins of the world. And the interesting thing about this historical account is those in the crowd who yelled "Crucify! Crucify!" were the very ones that Jesus was dying for.

And the interesting thing about this historical account is those in the crowd who yelled "Crucify! Crucify!" were the very ones that Jesus was dying for. Though the people were blinded spiritually, and, in their depravity, they sought to extinguish the very Son of God, the great love of God and His everlasting mercies poured out from the cross so those very same people might have a way back to God. Today, we can envision being in a theater or a stadium where someone is marched in, stoned, electrocuted, or even given a lethal injection. Imagine a crowd of people looking on as the criminal breathed his last breath. They were the people, the sinners in the world who had fallen short of the glory of God. Jesus died so that sinners like you and me could be forgiven of our sins and be declared righteous in the sight of our Holy God.

A third observation, a third word, is *the provision*. They crucified Him at the place called Calvary. The people wanted Jesus killed, but then there was the provision, Jesus Christ, Son of God, on the cross. Here we find the great sacrifice of the Son of God punished for crimes He did not commit. Here we see Jesus Christ, the righteous one, innocent from all charges even according to Pilate, but being lifted onto the cross and suffering this penalty. Why did He do this?

The Bible tells us that He did this because of his great love for you and me. The message for the marketplace today in the twenty-first century is that Jesus Christ is the way, the truth, and the life. No man, woman, or child can come to the Holy God except through faith in Him. Though Jesus suffered, bled, and died on the cross, His death was not in vain. His provision was God's remedy for our sin and also for those out in the marketplace. Jesus said, "if I be lifted up I will draw all men to myself." On that day in history, Jesus Christ died on a cross as the mediator between the Holy God and sinners like you and me.

This is the gospel of Jesus Christ, and through this historical event, God accomplished our redemption. He redeemed us from our sins, and we are now presented as righteous through the righteousness of Jesus Christ. This was a great substitution in this provision of God. Jesus gave His life. No man took it. Jesus gave His life and took our sins to the cross so that you and I may have them removed and now be clothed in His glorious righteousness. When we could not go to God, He came to us on the cross. The provision of Jesus Christ was God's gift to humanity. He was as much a king on the cross as when He was born in a manger. He will be the same when He returns the second time in His glorious second advent.

There are those in the marketplace who have never heard of the biblical Jesus, and they do not understand the spiritual truths that flow from this historical account. Join me in taking the good news of Jesus Christ in His free grace and His provision on the cross to those in the marketplace who may never enter the doors of a church. We know Jesus died as God's provision for our sins. Then on the coming Sunday, God raised Him in glory in a victorious bodily physical resurrection. That stamped His approval upon the provision, the atonement of His Son for sinners such as you and me. How can it be that my God would die for me? We find it in this text. He did it because He loves you.

God bless you, my friend.

DAY 16

···✦✦✦✦···

*For the Lord Himself will descend from heaven with a shout, with
the voice of an archangel, and with the trumpet of God. And the
dead in Christ will rise first. Then we who are alive and remain
shall be caught up together with them in the clouds to meet the Lord
in the air. And thus we shall always be with the Lord. Therefore
comfort one another with these words.*

1 Thessalonians 4:16–18

*H*ere we find Paul's first letter to the Thessalonians. There
are two letters inspired in the canon, 1 and 2 Thessalonians
in the New Testament. In the book of Acts, the book of church
history, we find Paul and his time in Thessalonica. When you read
this account, you see his ministry in the marketplace created quite
a stir. He was accused of causing riots and chaos because he was
proclaiming the gospel of Jesus Christ in the marketplace. How
about that? It sounds like we need some of that in the United
States today. Amen?

Paul was with Jason, with whose household Paul was meeting
(Acts 17:5–9). Paul and his associates left while Jason was there to
stand before the magistrates and give an account for his surety or

his time with Paul. But Paul went on to the next place to preach the gospel. Here we find him returning to Thessalonica.

I want to share three observations from these familiar verses where Paul focuses on the return of Jesus Christ. That's right. Jesus Christ is coming again, dear friend. The only promises in the Word of God not yet fulfilled are those dealing with the Second Advent.

The first observation is Christ's return will be *a personal return*. Don't miss this, for the Lord Himself will descend from heaven. Years ago, when I was in the financial world and was interviewed for job positions or a special meeting invitation, someone would ask me to come and be a part of a working session. Many times, those who were in high leadership positions would send a representative to pick me up in a limousine. The drivers would say, "Mr. Hamlet. Here is your ride. We want to take you back to the meeting." I remember riding in the vehicle with anticipation. I was about to meet that person or persons I would be dealing with on important business matters. This earthy illustration can, in no way, state the magnificence of what it means to be personally attended to by Jesus Christ. It would have been a great honor if those businessmen had come. I could have enjoyed the conversation in the car heading to the meeting. The King of Kings, Jesus Christ, is not sending His representatives to bring us to Himself in that glorious time of the second coming. He is coming Himself.

Yes. There will be the angel's proclamation. The trumpet will sound. There will be shouts. All of that will happen, but the glorious part of the coming of Christ for His people the second time will be the personal return of Jesus. Are you ready for that time? Here is the good news. By His grace and through faith in Jesus Christ, we can be born again and grow in the grace and knowledge of Christ here in this earthly realm. We can be ready for His coming again. When Jesus spoke about the second coming in the gospel narrative, He said, "when the Son of Man comes, will He really find faith on the earth?" (Luke 18:8). Oh, dear friend, if Christ were to come today, would He find faith in our lives?

The second observation is that Christ's return will be *a profitable return*. Paul says in verse 17, "We who are alive and remain shall be caught up together with them in the clouds." This is after the dead in Christ rise. You know God is the creator of life. He can take dust and create Adam. He can take dust, remains, and bones and create new glorified physical bodies. That is what He will do on that day. The dead in Christ will have new bodies, but those who are alive when Christ comes again, whatever their generation, will not die. They will be like Enoch or Elijah. There will be a translation. There must be a change. The mortal must take on the immortal. This day is coming. It will be a profitable return because we will leave behind this world and those things that are dying, those things under the curse and the fall upon this earth, mankind, and the weight of wickedness that so easily snares us. Even as we grow in the grace of God, we will continue to struggle with the tension between the spirit and flesh in our daily lives. It will be a profitable return.

True profitability in kingdom business is having a product that does not decay and will never die. It is the immortal. The book of Hebrews says God is shaking the visible foundation so that we may place our trust and faith on that which cannot be shaken (Hebrews 12:27), that which is the invisible. But soon to be the visible manifestation of Christ coming again when He will right every wrong. The best is yet to come for the born again believer in Jesus Christ. Christ's coming will be a profitable return. It will be profitable for those who are redeemed by the blood. It will be profitable for our great God in heaven, for He will glorify himself. He will share His glory with no one else. On that day, the enemy will be brought under the feet of Christ once and for all.

Our third observation about the return of Christ is it will be *a permanent return*. Scripture says, "We shall always be with the Lord. Therefore, comfort one another with these words." Dear friend, there is a day coming when we will never be removed from the presence of Jesus Christ in His glorified body. We will never be removed again. It will be a permanent relationship of sight. We walk by faith, not by sight. Now, we have Christ's Spirit working in our hearts as believers, just as Jesus in His glorified body, the second person of the Trinity, who intercedes and advocates for us in the heavenly. On that day, this permanent return of Jesus Christ to be with His visible people, the shepherd, and the sheep will come together in a visible pasture for all of eternity. This is a day that should bring great hope to you and me as believers in Christ but hear me. Many in the marketplace are outside of Christ. Many do not know of this love and grace of God. Many do not know of the free pardon of sin that anyone can have by coming through a personal relationship with Jesus Christ through repentance, turning from sin, and trusting and clinging to Jesus Christ. It can happen today. There are those who can literally be born again today in the spiritual realm and join the everlasting throng of believers on this permanent return with Christ coming, and His people reconciled. It is a glorious truth today to know that just like the Thessalonians, we, as twenty-first century Christians in America and all around the globe, can look forward to the return of Christ. Let us live today like Christ is coming back tonight. Put off those things that are decaying and corruptible and today cling to that which is incorruptible. Jesus Christ is coming back. Are you ready to receive him? The marketplace needs to hear of this truth.

God bless you, my friend.

DAY 17

....+.+....

So Samuel did what the LORD said, and went to Bethlehem. And the elders of the town trembled at his coming, and said, "Do you come peaceably?"

And he said, "Peaceably; I have come to sacrifice to the LORD. Sanctify yourselves, and come with me to the sacrifice." Then he consecrated Jesse and his sons, and invited them to the sacrifice.

So it was, when they came, that he looked at Eliab and said, "Surely the LORD's anointed is before Him!"

But the LORD said to Samuel, "Do not look at his appearance or at his physical stature, because I have refused him. For the LORD does not see as man sees; for man looks at the outward appearance, but the LORD looks at the heart."

1 Samuel 16:4–7

*H*ere we are in the Old Testament in the book of First Samuel. This is a book of the history of God's people under the Old Covenant before the time of Jesus Christ. The prophet Samuel is ministering at that time in Israel. He had just experienced a very problematic situation. King Saul had disobeyed the revealed Word of God when God, through Samuel, had directed him to go and utterly destroy the Amalekites. Saul spared lives and goods and came back with his self-proclaimed type of worship to God. Samuel said, "The LORD has torn the kingdom of Israel from you today, and has given it to a neighbor of yours, who is better than you" (1 Samuel 15:28). Afterward, God directed Samuel to go to Bethlehem, and this is where we pick up in the portion of the reading today from Scripture.

God directed Samuel to go to Jesse's household and invite the family to a time of sacrifice. On that visit, God would show him who the next king or leader of Israel would be. Here are the three observations I want to share from these verses or within the context of 1 Samuel 16.

First, there's *God's choice*. When God spoke to Samuel, He very clearly said, "I am sending you to Jesse the Bethlehemite. For I have provided Myself a king among his sons" (1 Samuel 16:1). When Samuel came to Bethlehem and saw the seven sons of Jesse one by one, he asked God if this was the one? God would say no, that is not my choice. Perhaps Samuel began with the oldest son down to the youngest, or maybe from the largest, tallest, or the shortest. We do not necessarily know the order, but it was clear God had chosen that man or even what the institutional community of faith would not choose. That is what God continues to do in our day in the twenty-first century. During the church age and now this season of grace under the new covenant, God continues to choose men and women who are the least on the list of candidates

God continues to choose men and women who are the least on the list of candidates from an outward appearance or visible perspective. But it's not man's choice. It's not the church's choice. It's God's choice.

from an outward appearance or visible perspective. But it's not man's choice. It's not the church's choice. It's God's choice. God has placed the church here to confirm the gifts of those He is calling into different ministries, both within and outside, the church walls.

Secondly, not only was there God's choice but *God's criteria*. Notice in the Scripture God told Samuel in verse 7, "For man looks at the outward appearance, but the Lord looks at the heart." God's criterion for leaders within the kingdom of God is the internal or hidden parts of the heart or soul that man does not see from the outside. He does not look at the external as criteria for His choices. God looks at the heart where His inward work of grace moves in the lives of His people—from conversion through consecration. All the way to completion when we are glorified when Christ comes again. This criteria is a spiritual one, and each one is different in the marketplace today. There are so many who attend churches or may partake of mass. They are involved in programs, but there is a form of godliness that lacks power (2 Timothy 3:5). There can be external celebrations, participation, and ordinances in the church's sacraments, but the criteria are not external; it is the internal. It is the heart that has been circumcised spiritually, where God has given a new heart. Ezekiel prophesied in the Old Testament that the heart of stone has become a heart of flesh, meaning a heart that is alive to God spiritually. That is who David was, but Samuel needed God to lead him to that person because he could not determine who would meet those criteria from a human standpoint.

And then lastly, there's *God's confirmation*. There was an external affirmation. God led Samuel to Jesse's youngest son, shepherding among the sheep. God said this is my choice. Now confirm him with an external anointing. Under the Old Covenant, when leaders were raised up, there was an anointing of oil. However, the oil itself did not make them spiritual. That's voodoo, friend.

It's only God's grace and His Spirit that changes the soul through the work of grace, which is outwardly confirmed as those gifts and their fruit is observed. David is anointed here, and his brothers and father were, no doubt, surprised. But isn't that just like God? God does what the institutional church today says is not possible, not probable, or surely is not the will of God many times. Is your desire to have a heart bent toward God, a heart that wants to be an instrument in the marketplace, networking, and in relationship? Do you want to be the voice of Christ with those who need to hear the good news of Jesus Christ?

If you are reading this, you are qualified. Congratulations, you meet the prerequisite. For God is searching the hearts of men. Literally, the eyes of the Lord move throughout the entire earth looking to see whose hearts are loyal to Him. You can be like David in this generation. It does not matter if you are a have or have not. It does not matter if you are a who's who or a who's not, the most likely to succeed or the least. In God's economy, He has a choice, a criteria, and He confirms the fruits of His children's lives that they are redeemed and they are in a position to advance His kingdom in whatever they are called to do daily.

God bless you, my friend.

DAY 18

·⸱⬩✦⬩✦·⸱·

Shadrack, Meshach, and Abed-Nego answered and said to the king, "O Nebuchadnezzar, we have no need to answer you in this matter. If that is the case, our God whom we serve is able to deliver us from the burning fiery furnace, and He will deliver us from your hand, O king. But if not, let it be known to you, O king, that we do not serve your gods, nor will we worship the gold image which you have set up."

Daniel 3:16–18

*I*n the book of Daniel, the book of prophecy, which is also a book of history, we see three young Hebrew men who had gone from Jerusalem to Babylon in exile. They were friends of Daniel, who was raised up to authority within King Nebuchadnezzar's pagan government. Here we find a critical time when these three men were challenged for their faith in Jesus Christ. There are three observations I want to share with you that flow from these verses and within the whole chapter of Daniel 3, which deals with Nebuchadnezzar and this great image.

First, there was *a choice to be made.* These three Hebrew men were standing for something. Someone once said if you stand for nothing, you will fall for anything. Here are three men who were brought into exile. They were the cream of the crop of the Hebrews who came into this pagan land. They were educated, skilled, and trained. No doubt, the pagan leadership and the king wanted to use these men to further the kingdom of Babylon. There was one problem. These men would not bow to the king's idol. Oh, dear friend, it is so important to know the same choices that these three men made in their time are the same choices we face in the twenty-first century as born-again believers. We are part of a pagan society, just as they were. We live in a society that has become anti-Christ. Our culture is drifting further away from God and His truths revealed in the gospel, in His Word. Some would say we must change our positions. We must compromise. We must not preach or proclaim the true gospel because it may offend someone else. We need to be more tolerant of those who disagree with us. These three Hebrews, Shadrach, Meshach, and Abed-Nego, were willing to lose their lives because they stood for truth. They made a choice, and the choice was not to serve a false god.

You may be like me and think these guys were amazing. They were super believers, if you will. No, hear me today. These were three ordinary men whom God empowered and enabled to testify with the strength of the Lord of the truth of God. There was a choice to be made. These three men would not bow to Nebuchadnezzar and his image or his god. Instead, they would face the consequences that would come. As twenty-first-century Christians, we need the grace of God to know that when choices are made, we must hear from God first and then follow through

As twenty-first-century Christians, we need the grace of God to know that when choices are made, we must hear from God first and then follow through in obedience to what He has called us to do.

in obedience to what He has called us to do. There are those in the marketplace who maybe have never gone into a church. They have never pulled out a hymnal or never heard a choir, but hear me: they are watching you and me. We may be the only ones who can, through our choices, point them to the truth of Jesus Christ.

The second observation is there was *a cost to be paid*. The price is simple. These guys were willing to give their lives. They offered themselves as a living sacrifice, not just into service but really into martyrdom. They were willing to go to heaven from the furnace. They were willing to go be with God by faith because they knew that their god was a true God. They would not compromise or change their testimonies to accommodate those who were in authority over them. It's a heavy cost. We all have one life. We don't get another shot. This is not a dress rehearsal. We do not come back as another creature. We do not come back as some hovering spirit. We have one life, and it will soon pass, but only what is done for Jesus will last. *These* men knew this was a cost that would require their lives, but they were not going to shrink from their testimonies. As a result, they were used to proclaim God's grace and, on that side of the cross, the gospel of Jesus Christ.

The third observation is there was a *kingdom to be displayed*. Later, in this text, we find these men were in a hot oven where they should have been consumed. The flames were so hot, just coming near it killed some of those who guarded the flames.

God protected Shadrach, Meshach, and Abed-Nego. He insulated them, so they were unharmed. They did not even have the smell of smoke on their garments. How can that be? Let me tell you who got into the furnace with them. When Nebuchadnezzar looked in and saw these three men were not harmed, he saw a fourth man in the fire. The additional man, I believe, was Jesus Christ in a Christophany in the Old Testament, as the Son of God, the Son of Man. It was Jesus Christ who came beside them.

When you and I go through trials and tribulations, when we go through marketplace persecution or when we are misjudged, misread, and misunderstood—when everyone thinks we are one particular way. Still, they do not know the truth because they do not want to ask the right questions or do their research. We can be assured that Jesus Christ is with us during those times of trial and persecution. He will never forsake us. He will never leave us.

These three men saw that a kingdom would be displayed. It was this way because King Jesus was there with them. All the pagan world, from the king to the paupers, would know that the God of Israel is the true God. They would know that the Kingdom of God is coming to earth, and He is coming to earth through the king sending His messengers, declaring the Word of God, declaring the gospel to the ends of the earth. Oh, what an encouraging text that Jesus Christ is on display.

I ask you: how is the kingdom of God being displayed in your life and my life? Dear friend, the answer to that is only if King Jesus is exalted. It is only King Jesus who can display the gospel of Christ through our lives. Oh, dear friend, our words, actions, our lips, lives, all those things in the marketplace, is what our culture and our society need to hear and see. They need to see that we bow to only King Jesus. Jesus desires for those who are outside the kingdom to come in through repentance and faith. Jesus Christ came to save sinners. Jesus Christ came into the world on a rescue mission. He came to save the religious and the reprobate. The kingdom displayed in glory within the flames is God's Kingdom, which God uses to advance through your life and mine.

Are you willing to take the gospel and advance the kingdom in your space of influence? I pray today that you will say yes, and you will make the choice that these three men made. I will follow Jesus whatever the cost.

God bless you, my friend.

DAY 19

······+◆+·····

There was a man of the Pharisees named Nicodemus, a ruler of the Jews. This man came to Jesus by night and said to Him, "Rabbi, we know that You are a teacher come from God; for no one can do these signs that You do unless God is with him."

Jesus answered and said to him, "Most assuredly, I say to you, unless one is born again, he cannot see the kingdom of God."

Nicodemus said to Him, "How can a man be born when he is old? Can he enter a second time into his mother's womb and be born?"

Jesus answered, "Most assuredly, I say to you, unless one is born of water and the Spirit, he cannot enter the kingdom of God. That which is born of the flesh is flesh, and that which is born of the Spirit is spirit. Do not marvel that I said to you, 'You must be born again.' The wind blows where it wishes, and you hear the sound of it, but cannot tell where it comes from and where it goes. So is everyone who is born of the Spirit."

John 3:1–8

*H*ere we find a gospel conversation. A gospel conversation is very simply a conversation centered around Jesus Christ and

His saving work. Here we find Nicodemus, a religious man who approached the Lord Jesus and was interested in a theological discussion. Perhaps he wanted to discuss the Jewish religion and other things related to spirituality. After Nicodemus brings his question to Jesus in chapter two, the Lord gives him the brutal, real truth. Jesus tells him, "unless one is born again, he cannot see the kingdom of God."

There are three observations I want to share related to being born again from this passage.

First, there is the mystery of *being born again*. In verse 8, Jesus referred to the work of the Holy Spirit as being a mystery, as being something like the wind. We cannot see the wind. We cannot contain it, but we can observe the very workings of the wind. We can even hear the sound of the effect of wind. A mystery is simply a hidden truth or something that is not revealed to us in our finite understanding. The wind is a mystery because we are accustomed to touching, seeing, or using our senses to be fully engaged in life. A mystery comes when some of those things are disengaged, actually hidden from us.

Jesus describes the work of the Holy Spirit as being a mystery. In the marketplace, the Spirit of God is roaming, striving with flesh. We are still in a season of grace, which means the door of salvation is still wide open for anyone to come, anytime, anywhere if they will come to repentance and faith in Jesus Christ. As the Spirit of God roams and uses the Word of God that is proclaimed in the gospel, He is convicting of sin, righteousness, and judgment. We cannot see that from an outward standpoint. Two people could be listening to the same message.

We are still in a season of grace, which means the door of salvation is still wide open for anyone to come, anytime, anywhere if they will come to repentance and faith in Jesus Christ.

One comes under great conviction and comes to repentance and faith in Christ, while the other, through the hardening of their heart, stays in unbelief and rejects the free offer of salvation in Jesus Christ. It is a mystery, but the Bible says that being born again is not done from an earthly standpoint but must come from heaven. To be born again, we must not be born again on earth. Instead, we must be born again literally from heaven and the work of the Spirit as the gospel is proclaimed. We respond from our inner soul with trust in Jesus Christ.

The second observation is *being born again*. It is not only being born again, but it is also a miracle. Jesus was not describing another physical birth but a spiritual birth. When Nicodemus first heard Jesus describe the new birth, he took it literally from a physical perspective. What he heard was he would have to go back into his mother's womb and be born again on earth. At that point, he did not have the spiritual eyes to see that Jesus was talking about spiritual birth. It was not a birth that originated on earth, but it was a birth that came from heaven to earth through the gospel of Jesus Christ. During Jesus' ministry, He performed great miracles. He turned water into wine, gave sight to the blind, and hearing to the deaf. He healed blood diseases and the lepers. Jesus even raised some from the dead. The greatest miracle that can happen in someone's life, which is physically alive in this world, like Nicodemus was or anyone in the twenty-first century, is to be born again by the gospel of Jesus Christ. The mystics want to manufacture and mimic the miracles of God apart from the power and provision of our great God in heaven. Their works are all done in vain, and only Jesus Christ can destroy the works of the devil. Jesus said we must be born of water and the spirit. He was saying that we are born physically through the water as we come from our mother's womb, but we also must be born again spiritually, by the gospel of Jesus Christ.

Finally, the third observation is the *mandate of being born again.* Notice in these verses Jesus said twice, "you must be born again." Dear friend, that is an imperative from our Lord. There is no other option for a sinner to be made right with Holy God. We must be born again through the shed blood of Jesus Christ and His imputed righteousness given to us through faith. If there is another way for us to be saved or a plan B, Jesus would have never left heaven's glory and come to earth to take on our humanity so that our sinful flesh could be transformed, renewed, and reconciled to the Holy God. The mandate is simple. There must be transformation.

Today, dear friend, your only hope is to cry out for the mercy of God, to plead with Him to do something in you that you cannot do for yourself. This comes through a personal relationship with Jesus Christ. One can look on to Christ and live. We can understand the transformation from an earthly perspective. Picture the caterpillar that leaves its cocoon and gains its wings to fly. It is no longer a worm but transformed into a butterfly. It undergoes changes in nature.

Similarly, a tadpole in a pond one day becomes a frog and leaves its domain of the water. It begins to breathe oxygen. There is a transformation. Both of these simple illustrations show a transformation. How much greater work does God do in the life of a sinner, when through the mysterious and convicting work of the Holy Spirit, we can joyfully repent of our sins and believe in Jesus Christ? Friend, the marketplace is full of people who are walking dead. They are physically alive but are spiritually dead and like Nicodemus. They need to hear the gospel of Jesus Christ. They need to hear that the door of salvation is still open. This is a season of grace that whosoever shall call upon the name of the Lord shall be saved. That is what being born again means, to call upon Christ. No sinner in their depravity would ever call upon Christ unless the Spirit convicts them of sin and uses the Word of God proclaimed to bring transformation. We are born again not by corruptible seed but by the incorruptible Word of God which is the gospel of Jesus Christ. Join me in taking that gospel into the boardroom, community room, stadium, into the theater, and yes, into the church where many are still in their sin.

God bless you, my friend.

DAY 20

··•◆◆•··

Therefore we must give the more earnest heed to the things we have heard, lest we drift away. For if the word spoken through angels proved steadfast, and every transgression and disobedience received a just reward, how shall we escape if we neglect so great a salvation, which at the first began to be spoken by the Lord, and was confirmed to us by those who heard Him?

Hebrews 2:1–3

*H*ere we find a letter to the Hebrews. We are not sure who the human author was of this book. Some believe the apostle Paul or Apollos or possibly other writers in the first century were used by God to pen this letter, but regardless of the human author, we know the real author is the Holy Spirit.

In this text, we see God exhorting believers in the Hebrew community. These were what you would call "completed Jews" or those who came under the Old Covenant and yet believed in Christ as their Savior. This letter focuses on Jesus Christ and the essentials of the New Covenant. There are three words or observations that I want to share flowing out of verse 3 with that context. "How shall we escape if we neglect so great a salvation?"

"What is your exit strategy?" Everyone who comes into this world must have an exit strategy.

Dear friend, we could ask the question, "What is your exit strategy?" Everyone who comes into this world must have an exit strategy. We are all born into this world and breathe our first breath as soon as we leave our mother's womb. There is also the last day when we will give up our spirit, and we will die. Our spirit will leave our body, and that will be the last breath and the ultimate exit. Therefore, we all should have a strategy. You and I, everyone in the world today, should have a strategy for how we will leave this world.

Here are three fatal responses to the gospel resulting in an exit strategy that would not greatly value anyone.

The first word is *rebellion*. Rebellion means to reject the gospel intentionally. There are many through the ages after Adam, both in the Old Testament and throughout the New Testament, who have rebelled against the gospel. The Bible says that "the grace of God which brings salvation hath appeared on all men" (Titus 2:11). "For God so loved the world that He gave His only begotten Son, that whoever believes in Him should not perish but have everlasting life" (John 3:16). This is the blessing or the promise of the gospel. The gospel guarantees a successful and positive exit strategy from time into eternity.

Rebellion is when someone hears the gospel and intentionally rejects the claims of Christ. They intentionally say, "I do not believe that Christ is Lord, or that He is the savior of the world, and I do not believe that I need Him to be made right with God."

Dear friend in the marketplace, so many go about their daily activities and their businesses. They go about their affairs, social activities, family relationships; they hear the gospel and reject it. They reject it because they do not believe the gospel is important to their souls. May we all know that the gospel is the only way for a person to be made right with God. Jesus Christ alone is the mediator between holy God and sinful men.

The second word is *delusion*. Delusion is a way of escaping or running from God. This is not an intentional rebellion, but it is more like drifting. It could be what we call nominalism or solely focusing on the external activities and motion. This delusion may be found even within the visible church or faith community where all things are observed. Maybe it is found in the ordinances and sacraments, yet that person is not born again through the gospel of Jesus Christ. That is a delusion, we might say. Perhaps they exhibit an affinity with Christ, or an association with Christ, even an acknowledgment of Him. It's like Dr. Adrian Rogers would say so eloquently: "Those who are outward professors but they're not really inward possessors of the lord Jesus Christ" (*The Secret of Supernatural Living*). The exit strategy for those who are under a delusion has an outcome similar to those in rebellion. Unless a person is born again by the gospel, by grace through faith in Jesus Christ, there is no exit strategy leading to everlasting life.

We might call this casual Christianity or pagan Christianity. Here we are in the United States of America, and war faces our headquarters. We live in an area that was called "the Bible Belt." Many would say surely everyone who comes into this culture by birth, family, or genealogy is a Christian. Today we live in a counter-Christian culture. We live in a post-Christian culture. But hear me today. It can be pre-Christian again. We can pray that God would bring a gospel awakening to our communities. Delusion is like going to a doctor who has a solution for your illness. Suppose he said, "Well, here's your solution, but I'm going to pour some water in this remedy because I don't want it to taste so bad. I want it to be more accommodating." Would you prefer this watered-down solution to the undiluted cure?

Absolutely not. Can you take that to the next level for a moment, to dilute the gospel of Jesus Christ, which is the power of God unto salvation? It is possible to be in the marketplace, be in the sanctuary, be in Christendom, in the community, and have a form of godliness that lacks the power thereof (2 Timothy 3:5). Many in this community of Hebrew believers were exhorted to examine themselves and see they won the fight. Today you may be listening, and you may be a member of a church. You may have grown up in a Christian family. You may have been baptized or sprinkled. You may take the Lord's Supper. You might take ceremonial mass and attend church. Any dilution of the gospel leads to an exit strategy that is apart from God.

The final word is *procrastination*. Procrastination is a fatal response or a way of escape leading to death because it puts off until tomorrow what God has called us to do today. Dear friend, did you realize today is the day of salvation? Do you realize you are in the marketplace?

In our culture, in the stadiums and the coliseum, the museums and the theaters, people come and go like walking dead men and women because they put off until tomorrow what God has called them to do today. Salvation is of the Lord, but the Holy Spirit strives with flesh. I believe the Holy Spirit is still striving with men today, and I believe the Holy Spirit is at work convicting of sin, righteousness, and judgment. When the Holy Spirit, through the teaching of the gospel, convicts a sinner, He demands a response. Procrastination is a deadly escape. Have you repented of your sin and believed in the Lord Jesus Christ? If you are a believer today, this message needs to go to all the marketplace. God wants to mobilize you. I encourage you, we go together, whether across the street or around the world. We must have an exit strategy focused on the gospel of Jesus Christ.

God bless you, my friend.

DAY 21

·· • ✦ • ✦ ·· ·

Then they said one to another. "We are not doing right. This day is a day of good news, and we remain silent. If we wait until morning light, some punishment will come upon us. Now therefore, come, let us go and tell the king's household."

2 Kings 7:9

*T*he context of this verse was within the nation of Israel when Elijah was the prophet. Second Kings is a book of the history of God's people in the Old Testament, and we find here the enemy of Israel.

Syria had encamped around the city in Samarra. Four lepers are excluded from the city under the law of Moses where the lepers were declared to be unclean. These lepers were outside of the gate. This was a time of drought and famine in Israel. It looked like the world was coming to an end. We pick up with these four lepers at the gate and a decision they had made. They knew that if they went inside the gate, they would be kicked out of the city. There was no life for them there. They knew if they stayed outside the gate where they were meant to stay under the law of Moses, they would die of starvation. They made a third choice, the only one for their survival. It was a risk going out to the enemy camp of the Syrians and cast themselves upon their mercy, asking for food and water. In chapter 7, we see them going forth and to the enemy's camp. Miraculously the enemy had left. The Syrian army was no longer there, but they had left their tents, food, drink, clothes, and even their silver and gold. Can you imagine the look on these four lepers' faces? They had nothing and were literally in their last days before starvation or being murdered by the enemy when they saw this bounty of blessings.

The first observation is these four lepers found a *bounty of blessings*. Here is a picture of the lepers who were the least in their society. They were even excluded from the marketplace, yet they found food and necessities of life that even those in the king's household did not have—what a beautiful picture.

In Ephesians 1, the Bible says we are justified freely by His grace through the redemption in Jesus Christ and blessed in all spiritual places with the blessing of Jesus Christ. And so was the bounty of blessing found by these four lepers as they took the risk and cast themselves really upon their enemy's discretion. God providentially called the enemy to leave. I tell you; our God is a faithful God. That is the bounty of blessing that we see from this text.

Secondly, there is the observation that there was a *sin of silence*. Notice these beggars, these lepers, went into the camp full of abundance. They must have thought about the stain and continued to accumulate things for themselves without thinking of sharing with anybody else in the marketplace or their community. This may be a natural reaction because they were excluded from the community of faith due to their leprosy. They probably had some feelings of revenge or payback. You know what I am talking about. This may not have been the highest priority for them to go back and share this bounty of blessing with others who were starving during this dark time. They made an observation themselves, and they agreed they were not doing right. The sin of silence is something today that we must all wrestle.

God has placed us in the marketplace, trophies of His grace, to radiate Christ and share the light of the gospel in the darkness.

God has placed us in the marketplace, trophies of His grace, to radiate Christ and share the light of the gospel in the darkness. The sin of silence will always be a tension for us because we have a fear of rejection. Dear friend, Scripture tells us that faith comes by hearing and hearing by the word of God. When we look in the New Testament, we see that Jesus had another encounter with some lepers. Once, He healed a leper and told him to show himself to the priest and not tell anybody. The man went to the priest, and the Bible says the report spread throughout the land. Surely this man could not hold back the good news he had received, and so he was speaking out even when Jesus said to be quiet.

Later in the narrative of the gospel, there is an account where Jesus healed ten lepers. Of the ten lepers, only one came back. Jesus asked where the other nine were who should be proclaiming this good news. They should not be silent in sharing. This is the sin of silence. I came to bring good news. My church must be the one that shares the gospel to each, end-all, in the marketplace.

Finally, we find the *wonder of witnessing*. In this verse, we read, "if we wait until morning light some punishment will come upon us. Now therefore, come, let us go and tell the king's household." Here they made the decision. This was intentional in this scene. For Jesus Christ, there must be intentionality. Therefore, we must pray to God before we ever proclaim the gospel without God's

Spirit anointing the proclamation. As the words go out, they can fall on hard hearts. We must intentionally decide and commit that each day, we are going to seek out gospel conversations. We must understand that God has divine appointments. He has prepared appointments for those in the marketplace who need to hear of Jesus Christ. God has prepared us to go forth for that time as we rely on the ministry of the Holy Spirit in our witnesses.

Here we see the paupers going back to share the good news. We see the castoffs, the lepers going to share with the king. The king was dying of starvation like the others. The nation was on its last leg, surrounded by the Syrian army. It looked like doomsday. Where would they find the good news or where they could find survival and food and drink? It would be from these four lepers who were cast out from their community. Isn't that just like God? The Bible says that when we come to faith in Christ, we are a new creature, and our friends, those who are enemies, are those who persecute us. We are to love them. It is impossible to love them and share with them the good news unless Christ is in us. Here we see a picture or an illustration of what it means to be a witness in the marketplace. The wonder of witnessing is that God can use the least in our society and marketplace to share the gospel with those in the highest positions of authority.

This brings to mind a man in Africa. Ginger and I were there several years ago preaching the gospel and teaching the national pastors. We were there during a time of civil war when the State Department was warning Americans not to go, but we felt led to go. God blessed that time and protected us by providing a man within the government who was a Daniel. This man came to faith in Christ out of his tribalism. God was using him even within that chaotic government. God had placed him in the king's court, if you will, taking him from his miry clay and his tribalism to now sharing the good news of Jesus Christ. There were government officials who were pagans coming to faith in Christ and being born again. Dear friend, God is doing this all around the world. May He use us as He anoints our lips anoints our lives.

God bless you, my friend.

DAY 22

· · ◆ ◆ ◆ ◆ · ·

Though the fig tree may not blossom,
Nor fruit be on the vines;
Though the labor of the olive may fail,
And the fields yield no food;
Though the flock may be cut off from the fold,
And there be no herd in the stalls—
Yet I will rejoice in the LORD,
I will joy in the God of my salvation.

The LORD God is my strength;
He will make my feet like deer's feet,
And He will make me walk on my high hills.

Habakkuk 3:17–19

*H*ere we find the prophet Habakkuk in the Old Testament. He lived in the nation of Judah during a dark time. His message for the people was a message from God. They needed to repent and forsake their idolatry and infidelity and their following after other gods. God had given the message to His prophet that a day of judgment was coming, and the Babylonians would come and destroy the city of Jerusalem, taking the Jews captive in a far land. There are three words or observations that I want to share from today's verses.

The first word is *adversity* from verse 17. Did you notice the language the prophet used? It was one of loss. It was one of setbacks and difficulties dealing with agriculture. The trees were not blossoming, and fruit was nowhere to be found on the vines. The livestock would no longer be in the barns and crops would fail their fields. It was a time of desperation, a time of decay and darkness. The word *adversity* brings to mind those things that happen in this generation within this visible community of faith and things that happen today. Today, we live in a fallen world where things are not getting better. Instead, they are getting worse. The culture has become more anti-gospel and more anti-Christian, unbiblical and immoral, This pagan culture seeks to extinguish the Gospel witness within the visible community of faith in our day.

Hear me today. Though the prophet was given this word as a revelation about the coming judgment upon the nation of Judah, there was also a soberness that God was still sovereign and on the throne. Within the context of this chapter, God was in effect purifying and going to remove the malignancy of unbelief that had grown and infected the nation of Judah. Friend, as we look at the marketplace today and see the ordinary affairs of our lives, many adversarial things happen. Some will oppose us because we are followers of Jesus Christ. Some will reject us because they worship other gods. Others will try to extinguish our witness because we are voices of the God of the Bible and we proclaim the gospel of Jesus Christ. This adversity was coming upon this generation because of their sin of unbelief.

We must be mindful today that adversity comes into our lives

We are voices of the God of the Bible and we proclaim the gospel of Jesus Christ.

many times because we have unconfessed sins and things that are not pleasing to God. We must remember that according to the Scripture, God chastises those He loves (Hebrews 12:6). He is in the process of conforming you and me as born again believers into the image of his precious son, Jesus Christ. This adversity, this loss of property and possessions, of crop yield was something forthcoming. The prophet Habakkuk did not mince any words in this graphic description.

The second word or observation from this passage is *doxology* in verse 18. After listing these specific setbacks within the agricultural language of that day, Habakkuk now pivots to a time of praise. The word *doxology* simply means to praise God through the ages. The redeemed of the Lord have proclaimed the goodness of God, His longsuffering and everlasting mercies. They proclaim His desire for reconciliation among those who had enmity with Him in each fallen generation. The prophet praises the Lord here and rejoices in the truth that it is God who has redeemed. It is God who saves His people and God who reconciles depraved sinners unto Himself through the liberating and life-giving gospel of Jesus Christ. On that side of the cross, they were looking for the promise of the coming of Jesus. Today we look back at the finished work of Christ.

We look back at His completed redemptive work. No matter what adversary, illness, opposition, or enemy attacks come our way—whether external or internal, whether enemies of Christ or because of our sinfulness, there should be a doxology in our lives that we know it is God who rules and reigns from above. It is God who is working out His purpose in the lives of His people. It is God pursuing sinners. He pursues those who are idolaters, those who are in unbelief, those who are spiritual adulterers in our generation today. Jesus Christ and His gospel can save to the uttermost those who will repent of their sins and believe on the Lord Jesus Christ.

The third word or observation is *durability*. In verse 19, the Scripture says, "the LORD God is my strength; He will make my feet like deer's feet, and He will make me walk on my high hills." Remember, this is within the context of a pending judgment. This is within the context of God chastising His people. Here we are in the concluding verses of this book of prophecy, and we find the conclusion dealing with durability, resilience, strength, and longevity. To the human mind, this seems to be the opposite way this inspired letter would close. This is a benediction and should be an encouragement to you and me, that as God was the strength of this prophet Habakkuk and of those who were the truly redeemed in that Old Testament time. Today in our godless generation and pagan world, there is a promise that God will be our strength. He has begun a good work in you and will perform it unto the day of Jesus Christ. As that doxology in the book of Jude declares, "Now to Him who is able to keep you from stumbling, and to present you faultless before the presence of His glory with exceeding joy" (Jude 24).

Oh, today may we run to the God of the Bible. May we run to our heavenly Father through the Lord Jesus Christ, and may we go and tell others in the marketplace, outside the church walls, that there is a God who is alive, and He is a God who is redeeming those who have sinned against Him. It is His love, mercy, and goodness that is calling sinners to come to Him. May we declare this message of hope even within the darkness of our pagan culture today.

God bless you, my friend.

DAY 23

···✦✦✦✦✦···

Jesus spoke these words, lifted up His eyes to heaven, and said: "Father, the hour has come. Glorify Your Son, that Your Son also may glorify You, as You have given Him authority over all flesh, that He should give eternal life to as many as You have given Him. And this is eternal life, that they may know You, the only true God, and Jesus Christ whom You have sent. I have glorified You on the earth. I have finished the work which You have given Me to do. And now, O Father, glorify Me together with Yourself, with the glory which I had with You before the world was."

John 17:1–5

*I*n the Gospel of John, we find the real Lord's Prayer. That's right. This was the Lord Jesus, God's Son, praying to His heavenly Father in the last hours before He would go to the cross to die for the sins of the world. Many look at the model prayer in Matthew 6 as the Lord's Prayer, but that was the Lord teaching us *how* to pray. There are two observations I want to share with you from these verses, but we really focus on verse three today.

The first observation is that *the gospel is about life, not death.* Throughout the civilizations of man, since the Garden of Eden, when man fell, the stench of death has rested upon society. The marketplace is full of aromas that were not of life but of death. Here we see the Lord Jesus talking about Himself, the gospel, and His heavenly Father. He speaks all about life. You see, life is something that must come from God. Only God can create life, and only He could breathe life into a person in the Garden of Eden. When God created the world, He formed man from the dust, and though man was of statue, there was no life until God breathed upon Him. Of course, that man was Adam. We know that Adam was the first man, coming to life when God breathed life into him. The prophet Ezekiel, during his day, had a vision of the dry bones of the dead. It was a place of decay, a place of destruction, like a cemetery where He faithfully proclaimed the Word of God. It was not until God's Spirit breathed upon those dry bones that there was life again. Oh, dear friend, hear me today. The only hope for the marketplace, the only hope for any person who is physically alive today, is that they experience life through the gospel of Jesus Christ. There are so many with agendas, life plans, and career paths, and all of those things will ultimately lead to death if there is not the life of God breathing upon a person through the saving gospel of Jesus Christ.

The second observation is *the gospel is not a religion* but a relationship. Notice in verse 3, that this eternal life is "that they may know you, the only true God and Jesus Christ [whom] you have sent." A relationship requires two parties, and here God, the Son, was praying to God, the Father, in His last days. He had a relationship and the Trinity. The gospel is about a relationship that, you and I, being created in the image of God, is tarnished and perverted by the fall and our sin. We need a restored relationship with our Holy God, which comes through the person of Jesus Christ.

Religion is what man creates as a way of trying to achieve merit, to satisfy the demands and the requirements of a deity they

Christianity is about a relationship, not a religion. It is about life, not death. And lastly, it is about eternity, not just history. don't know. As Jesus was praying in John 17, Biblical Christianity is about a relationship where God the Son came from heaven down to earth to accomplish the work of redemption for sinners like us.

That is why we read in verse 4, that He has "finished the work that [God] has given [Him] to do." What work did God the Father give God the Son to do in His life on earth as the Son of Man? It was to accomplish God's redemptive work and consummate that great reconciliation that bridged the gap between holy God in heaven and man on earth.

I refer you to the cross a few hours later where Jesus, in His last breath said, "it is finished" (John 19:30). Was He saying this is my last religious effort? Was He saying this is the end of the hope for man? No. He was saying that He had finished the redemptive work. His blood was shed for you and me to establish a relationship that comes through repentance and faith in Jesus Christ Himself. Christianity is about a relationship, not a religion. It is about life, not death. And lastly, it is about eternity, not just history.

Jesus Christ was, and is, a real person who lived and walked this earth for approximately thirty-three years in the Middle East and around Jerusalem. Many people study Christianity, the Gospels, or the Bible from only a historical perspective. They look back and say, look what God did in the past. Let's increase our intellectual assent or mental library about what happened in history regarding religion or Jesus Christ.

Oh, dear friend, hear me today. The gospel is a historical account based on the person and work of Jesus Christ, but it deals more with eternity than history. History is a part of eternity. The past is part of eternity. Eternity is forever. That is why the Bible is called the everlasting gospel. It does not come and go based on a capsule of time or based on some calendar of history. It is about Jesus Christ, the everlasting God coming to earth to save sinners like you and me, whose souls will live forever in either a place called heaven or hell. Jesus Christ came to bring about eternal life. This is eternal life. The Scripture says, "that they may know you." Eternal life is found through the personal relationship we have as sinners with Jesus Christ in His redemptive work.

We are sinners who are born again by the gospel, and we become saints. We become renewed. We become justified, sanctified, and one day will be glorified. Oh, dear friend, this should excite you today. There are those in the marketplace who are one heartbeat away from meeting God, the judge of the universe. They need to hear the gospel that Jesus died for them. They need to hear that they can spend eternity with God in heaven, but it must start with a personal relationship through faith in Christ today.

God bless you, my friend.

DAY 24

．．＋＋◆＋・・

Beloved, do not believe every spirit, but test the spirits, whether they are of God; because many false prophets have gone out into the world. By this you know the Spirit of God: Every spirit that confesses that Jesus Christ has come in the flesh is of God, and every spirit that does not confess that Jesus Christ has come in the flesh is not of God. And this is the spirit of the Antichrist, which you have heard was coming, and is now already in the world.

1 John 4:1–3

*H*ere we find the apostle John writing this letter in his latter days under the inspiration of the Holy Spirit. This is the same apostle John who walked with Jesus in the flesh, who was so close to him during his earthly ministry. In the book of first John, we find three observations that flow practically to where we are in our twenty-first century marketplace.

There are and were *religious spirits*. Religious spirits are those spirits or intentions in the marketplace, even within church cathedrals and sanctuaries, where there is this effort, this thrust of man trying to work his way to Holy God.

Can you picture that for just a moment? You are born again by the grace of God in the gospel of Jesus Christ. You trust in Christ's righteousness. You can now see what you didn't see between holy God and sinful man. You see, there would be no way that the works of the flesh could ever justify a man before God—the works of the law, religion, deeds, or outward ceremonies. The world is full of religious spirits today, and they were present during this time in the first century when John wrote this epistle. These spirits are everywhere, even within pagan marketplaces. Here we are in the United States, where many who came to our country believed in the Word of God. They believed in the gospel and freedom of religion, freedom of speech, and separation of church and state. They believed the state should not govern the church. Now, almost two hundred fifty years later, in the United States, we are in a time where many religious spirits have nothing to do with Jesus Christ. Our country is great because it is a democracy, and there is freedom for every person to believe what they choose to believe and worship how they want to worship. Hear me today. Christ's church in America must recognize that religious spirits are trying to detour and divert those in the marketplace to trust in their own works instead of believing in Jesus Christ alone and being born again. May we watch out and be careful. That is an anti-Christ spirit. Yes. Christianity is not primarily a religion, hear me, it is a relationship. Any spirit that points to anything else outside of the merit of Jesus Christ and his righteousness, is an anti-Christ spirit.

Christianity is not primarily a religion, it is a relationship.

In the second observation, we see *cultural spirits* now flowing out of the context. In John's time, you can just sense that the religious spirits were there, but there were also cultural spirits. The cultural spirits are those intentions and passions coming from people who are misled. We see this in how the culture is becoming wider and deeper with many philosophies that the Bible calls vain traditions. There is just a plurality of cultural things driven not by the gospel but by society and things that are happening and reacting to circumstances. Dear friend, today, a cultural spirit is an anti-Christ spirit if it is against the revelation of Scripture. If it is against crisis and anti-Christ spirit, then it is against a biblical worldview. What is a biblical worldview? Good question. Here's the easy answer. A biblical worldview is a view of the world that is biblical. It is simple to see the world today, in our twenty-first century culture, as well as in the marketplace, that cultural spirits are prodding and pulling helpless souls who are outside of Christ. These cultural spirits pull them into a destiny of eternal death because they have chosen to reject Christ and His gospel. May we perceive and discern those religious spirits and cultural spirits, which are both anti-Christ and anti-gospel. May we be the salt and light of God. May we be on fire for the gospel in the marketplace and proclaim Christ.

The third observation is the *materialistic spirits* within our culture. Materialism has become an idol. Materialism has always been a great temptation for fallen man. We find it throughout the Scripture in both the Old and New Testaments when there is gain in material resources. God gives every person the ability to create wealth and earn a living. Within materialist spirits, we see the creature man worshipping other creatures. The creation and materialistic spirit is also an anti-Christ spirit.

John tells us to test every spirit. Many today in Christendom have blended this materialism and prosperity into the purity and simplicity of the gospel. Jesus Christ came to save sinners. He came to save souls, and though the gospel is holistic for the body, soul, and spirit, one day we will have redeemed bodies glorified through Christ. Like Him, through His gospel on earth in this fallen world, materialistic spirits are tempting us. They are all around us, and we as Christ's church, must arise. We must discern these materialistic spirits. We must see that idolatry happens whenever we put anything in this creation or any other creature ahead of Jesus Christ in our life. The apostle John is exhorting us today in the marketplace. Watch out, discern those spirits and intentions, those passions pointing us to becoming self-made men and women to build our businesses, and yet neglect the business of the kingdom made today. May we each be exhorted in this matter.

May we each see the opportunity to witness to those affected by these anti-Christ spirits in the marketplace. May we be the kernel of truth. May we be the voice of God. May we be the ones who ask, "Have you considered the claims of Jesus Christ?" I tell you. God can use anybody, anytime, anywhere. Are you available? If you are reading this today, you are qualified because you are a common person, an ordinary man or woman, and God can do extraordinary things with you as you are in your marketplace. You are pointing people to Jesus Christ in His redemptive work.

God bless you, my friend.

DAY 25

····◆·◆·◆··◆·····

O LORD our God, all this abundance that we have prepared to build You a house for Your holy name is from Your hand, and is all Your own. I know also, my God, that You test the heart and have pleasure in uprightness. As for me, in the uprightness of my heart I have willingly offered all these things; and now with joy I have seen Your people, who are present here to offer willingly to You. O LORD God of Abraham, Isaac, and Israel, our fathers, keep this forever in the intent of the thoughts of the heart of Your people, and fix their heart toward You. And give my son Solomon a loyal heart to keep Your commandments and Your testimonies and Your statutes, to do all these things, and to build the temple for which I have made provision.

1 Chronicles 29:16–19

*F*irst Chronicles is a book of history that parallels the books of 1 and 2 Kings. They contain the history of God's people from more of a political standpoint. First and Second Chronicles record roughly the same time period from a religious point of view, although they intermingle in so many ways within the history of Israel and the record of events where we find the context.

King David is about to pass the baton of leadership to his son, Solomon, as his days are nearing an end. God told David that He wanted his son to build the temple. David was not allowed to build a temple because the Bible says he was a man of war. In David's journey of faith, we see that he has many ups and downs, which you and I can identify with today. He had his good days and bad, but he was a man after God's own heart.

In this passage, David is showing his biblical leadership. The people, in a congregation, come together and offer their possessions, the things that they had from the work of their hands to God to be used toward the furnishings for His temple that would be built later. There are three observations I want to share out of these verses.

The first. *God is the source.* Notice in verse sixteen David said, Lord, what we are giving to you today is from you. You realize this is true in any believer's life, of every person who believes in Christ and who is born again by the gospel of Jesus Christ. God is the source of all blessings. The same truth applies even to the unregenerate, who are outside of Christ and need to be born again by the gospel. Everything that they have is from God. The source of everything in this world comes from God as a Creator. Every person born of Adam has a relationship with God, whether saved or not, as being one who God has enabled in heaven.

David, who was on that side of the cross, and the people of God there who were truly committed followers of God in the Old Testament, could say, *Yes God, You are my source not only of every physical blessing but You are the source of every spiritual blessing.* Today, can you see the blessings of God and Jesus Christ? Can you see that all of the things in Jesus Christ are yes and amen? Can you see that your next breath is because God is your source? Am I living my life keeping short accounts? Are we dying daily? Do we understand that God is our provider? He is our protector. Let us follow David's example as he did in this assembly of the people as they consecrated their possessions to the furnishing of the temple. Let us acknowledge God. Everything we have, our life, our breath, everything is all from God, so we give it back to Him.

The second observation is in verse 17. *God is not only our source, but He is the subject.* Notice in this prayer, David is proclaiming and declaring. He is saying everything God gives us, we give back to God. This is not a spiritual grammar lesson. There is basic grammar here. Jesus Christ, His gospel, and God the triune is the subject of everything that we do now. He is the object of what we do. He is the predicate of what we do in the sense that everything we do flows to Him and for Him. But, dear friend, He is the Alpha and the Omega. He is the beginning and the end. David was saying that everything we are giving here, out of the uprightness of our heart, is given to You, God. We give it willingly. You are the source. You've given us all these blessings. We are responding to You because You are the subject of our praise. The Bible says God has created all things for His glory. Revelation says, there around the throne in those last days, will be that song to God that God You are worthy for You have created all things and all things have been created for Your pleasure (4:11). That's what David was doing here.

The third observation is in verse 18. God is not only the source and the subject, *God is the sanctified.* That word sanctification means *to be set apart.* We often think of sanctification, and rightfully so, as something we do within ourselves to consecrate ourselves. The Bible says we are to be sanctified, to be set apart.

I want to tell you this, sanctification in us comes from God. We can do nothing in our own sanctification unless God works in us and through us according to His will and good pleasure. You and I cannot live the Christian life just by having good intentions, just by trying to keep biblical resolutions, or just by doing things every day on a principle basis, or even just by following Christ and His teachings. We need God to sanctify and define us. We must have the Lord working in and through us. The apostle Paul declared in 1 Thessalonians 5:23, "may the God of peace Himself sanctify you completely; and may your whole spirit, soul, and body be preserved blameless at the coming of our Lord Jesus Christ." What was he saying to that New Testament congregation? He was saying we are to grow in the grace and knowledge of Jesus Christ, and we are to grow in our body, soul, and spirit. We are to be set apart in the way we live.

Our life here is preparing us for the next world when we die. When we close our eyes on earth, we will open our eyes before Christ. It is a transition. It is not the end. It is only the beginning of the rest of eternity.

David possessed that heart of eternity. He yearned for the presence of God. David yearned for that day when there would be no more sin. He had times when he fell short. He had to repent with his time with Bathsheba. He was a murderer. He was an adulterer, but, by the grace of God, he was sanctified, and until his last breath, he gave willingly to God. Here he was leading the people.

How did these people look to him as a leader, having seen his failures before and the times that he made some bad decisions or some judgment calls that were not exactly right? God pruned and filtered David. Here they are before him still acknowledging that he was a man after God's own heart. He was a man who was a work in progress. I ask you today, are you like David? Do we believe that God is continuing to sanctify us and work out his life living in and through us? Is Jesus Christ being formed in us today? That was David's prayer and the prayer of the people. It should be your prayer today.

Dear friend, let us go into the marketplace. Let us go where the crowds are. Let us go to the theaters and stadiums. Let us go into the streets and the highways and byways and declare that Jesus Christ alone is worthy. Let us declare that Jesus died for the nations to declare that He is Jesus Christ. He is the source of life. He is the subject of life, and He is the one that was formed in us through the gospel. Will you join me as we take the everlasting gospel into the marketplace within our sphere of influence? May we be filled with the Spirit of God and go forth in the army of our Lord.

God bless you, my friend.

DAY 26

· · + + ◆ + + · ·

*Now the word of the LORD came to Jonah the second time, saying,
"Arise, go to Nineveh, that great city, and preach to it the message
that I tell you." So Jonah arose and went to Nineveh, according to
the word of the LORD. Now Nineveh was an exceedingly great city,
a three-day journey in extent. And Jonah began to enter the city on
the first day's walk. Then he cried out and said, "Yet forty days,
and Nineveh shall be overthrown!"*

*So the people of Nineveh believed God, proclaimed a fast, and put
on sackcloth, from the greatest to the least of them.*

Jonah 3:1–5

*H*ere we find Jonah, who was a prophet in the Old Testament.
His book might be referred to as a minor prophecy book, but
he had a major message. Though only four chapters, God called
this man to preach His Word to those who had not heard of His
love, to those who were outside the commonwealth of Israel. Jonah
was a Hebrew evangelist and was no doubt comfortable within his
environment, within the kingdom of Israel. However, there came
a day when God told him to you to go to Nineveh and preach the

Word. In chapter one, Jonah decided to go in the other direction. He rebelled against God's will and went to Tarsus. As a result, God brought a storm and Jonah was thrown off the boat by the sailors. A fish then swallowed him. For three days, he was in the belly of the fish, but God was merciful and called to the fish to spew him out onto the shore. Now, here we are in chapter three, and the Word of the Lord came to him again. The Lord is merciful, dear friend. Jonah was a messenger of God who had the message of God, and God was going to use him. He was not finished with him. He was a work in progress.

The first observation I want to share with you is, *there was God's message*. The Word of the Lord came to Jonah. The Word of the Lord is when God speaks to us. We have His Word, the Bible. It is His inspired, infallible, and inherent Word. God speaks to us today through the Bible, but this time He spoke verbally to Jonah.

He said, "Jonah, I want you to go to proclaim my goodness and my truth to the Ninevites. I created them in my image, just like I created you. They may have a different pigmentation of the skin, and they might not speak Hebrew. They may speak Persian. They may be different from you in their social classes, but they came from one blood just as you did. Everybody came from Adam."

We see this in the message of God. It is the Word of God. This is the gospel of Jesus Christ, and it is no different than in today's marketplace. The marketplace needs to hear the Word of God.

There are so many false gospels and messages from man's wisdom, maybe even from religious institutions, but the authenticity of the gospel must be proclaimed. It is God's pure message. It is God's message of salvation, and God told Jonah to go to Nineveh and preach to them (or proclaim to them) "My" word. First, there is God's message.

Second, I want you to see God's messenger. *God's message is always perfect*. His gospel is the everlasting gospel. It is age to age the same, but Jonah and you and I are not perfect as messengers. I mentioned how he had disobeyed God initially, but God gave him a second opportunity, a second chance, if you will, to be obedient.

This is where we pick up in this text. Jonah was given a second chance to proclaim the Word of God in Nineveh. His message was very simple. He was to preach whatever God gave him to preach. We are no different today as messengers of God than Jonah. We must proclaim God's Word and not our own words. Jonah was a man who finally got it right. He was an expositor if you will. He was preaching the message of God. We do not have the outline here of his message. We do not have his manuscript, but we know that God sent him to preach His Word.

Like Jonah, we are His messengers, and we have no other message but God's. There are many great preachers, teachers, counselors, and witnesses around Christianity in our generation. There are many in the marketplace, and some may even be listening today and saying, "Well, I am not called to preach. I am not called even to vocational ministry. I understand Jonah's calling. He was a messenger, and he preached God's message." You may be asking, "How does this apply to me?" That is a great question, friend because whether we are in the pulpit, in the pew, the sanctuary, or in the stadium, it is time to be a messenger of God. It is time to be God's spokesman, his agent. We are the mouth of God as we proclaim the Word of God.

I am not talking about just public proclamation within great assemblies. God may not call you to do that. I am talking about personal gospel conversations, one-on-one or in small groups, sharing the message of God, which is His glorious gospel. Jonah was God's messenger. He went to the city of Nineveh, which would be like New York City today. The Bible says it was a three-day journey. Can you imagine walking around the periphery of this city? Here is a guy who was a Jewish racist. He was not happy to be there.

We must be the mouth of God. We need to advance God's kingdom. We need to be a sphere of influence because it is God's time, and He has delayed His judgment and His return so that more could hear the gospel, and more could be saved as He draws them into our message.

He really did not want to preach God's message and be faithful as God's messenger because he knew that God was mighty to save, and that God would bless His Word by His Spirit. He knew there would be those who would come to repentance and believe in Christ on that side of the cross. Jonah knew that, but he continued in his faithfulness, maybe in his bad attitude, as we see later in this book. But he proclaimed that judgment is coming different today in the marketplace. There has never been a time greater than now in the twenty-first century and in a post-Christian postmodern society. We must be the mouth of God, and we must proclaim His Word. We need to advance God's kingdom. We need to be a sphere of influence because it is God's time, and He has delayed His judgment and His return so that more could hear the gospel, and more could be saved as He draws them into our message.

The third observation is *God's mercy.* Verse five gives us the conclusion or the outcome of the fruit of God's message preached through His messenger Jonah. The Bible said when the people of Nineveh heard it, they believed in God. They proclaimed a fast and put on sackcloth from the greatest to the least of them. This must have been an awesome time. Wouldn't you have liked to have been there with God's Word being proclaimed? To see and hear His messenger being faithful in the marketplace, in the streets around this great urban center, and seeing those who heard the Gospel repented. The fruit of their salvation came forth. Oh, dear friend, listen. Scripture tells us they fasted and put on sackcloth.

That would be a meritorious work if they were trusting in that. But they did not trust in that. They trusted in God. They repented, and the Bible says they believed in God. Because we believe in God and are saved by grace through faith through Christ alone, there will be fruits of the gospel. There will be a response and an inward change. Here we see the people of Nineveh responding outwardly because their hearts were melted.

Dear friend, I want to encourage you. There are those in the marketplace who may be pluralistic. They may be pagans. They may have an Eastern religion. They may have a Western religion, but dear friend, what they need, like those in Jonah's time, is messengers like Jonah. These messengers are you and I proclaiming the gospel and earning the right to have relationships of sharing Christ, to share gospel nuggets, and gospel conversations. We must rely on the Spirit of God, but God is mighty to save in the marketplace just like He was in the marketplaces of Nineveh. God bless you, my friend.

DAY 27

···◆◆◆···

Then Saul, still breathing threats and murder against the disciples of the Lord, went to the high priest and asked letters from him to the synagogues of Damascus, so that if he found any who were of the Way, whether men or women, he might bring them bound to Jerusalem.

As he journeyed he came near Damascus, and suddenly a light shown around him from heaven. Then he fell to the ground, and heard a voice saying to him, "Saul, Saul, why are you persecuting Me?"

And he said, "Who are you Lord?"

Then the Lord said, "I am Jesus, whom you are persecuting. It is hard for you to kick against the goads."

So he, trembling and astonished, said, "Lord, what do You want me to do?"

Then the Lord said to him, "Arise and go into the city, and you will be told what you must do."

And the men who journeyed with him stood speechless, hearing a voice but seeing no one. Then Saul arose from the ground, and when his eyes were opened he saw no one. But they led him by the hand and brought him into Damascus. And he was three days without sight and neither ate nor drank.

Acts 9:1–9

*T*his passage is known as the conversion experience of Saul. Saul was a Pharisee, a religious leader in Israel who opposed the gospel of Jesus Christ. He was trained in the Old Testament law, prophets, other writings, and other traditions of Judaism. He was convinced that he was absolutely right in his religious convictions and that this man, Jesus Christ, who was crucified on a cross in Jerusalem, was a fraud and was not who He claimed to be—the Son of the Living God. As you know, the book of Acts is the book of church history. The early church flowed out of Jerusalem and spread to the nations. God had chosen a specific person to be the apostle to the Gentiles and the pagans outside Israel. And, yes, that man's name was Saul. There are three words or observations that I want to share out of the text today.

First is the word *persecution*. Now, as we read in the text, Jesus confronted Saul with this question, "Why are you persecuting Me?" What an interesting question to come from the Lord Jesus as He pursued Saul on his way to Damascus to apprehend Christians. The word persecution means hostility, opposition, or enemy attacks. Jesus was very direct in this question to Saul, a religious man, a Pharisee from the nation of Israel. Jesus asked, "Why are you persecuting Me?" Different persecution in the Christian faith happens when those who oppose the gospel attack those who are fully committed followers of Jesus Christ. It happened during these early church days in Jerusalem right after Christ's death, burial, resurrection, and ascension and continued with the church's expansion at Pentecost.

But friend, it is happening today. I know many of you have seen the videos on television and social media of those around the world who are followers of Christ martyred by other religious fanatics and extremists who hold to their religious convictions and are opposed to the gospel of Jesus Christ. Even within the United States of America, within *our* country, there is persecution from anti-Christ spirits that are not only in the marketplace but are also in the visible church. Demonic forces seek to extinguish and quiet those voices and stop the advances of the gospel because the world, the flesh, and the devil hate the gospel and Jesus Christ.

The second observation or word is *apprehension*. In this context, Jesus apprehended Saul. In other epistles in the New Testament, Saul (later known as Paul) elaborates more on this matter of apprehension. In the book of Philippians, Paul (formerly Saul) declared,

> Not that I have already attained, or am already perfected; but I press on, that I may lay hold of that for which Christ Jesus has also laid hold of me. Brethren, I do not count myself to have apprehended; but one thing I do, forgetting those things which are behind and reaching forward to those things which are ahead, I press toward the goal for the prize of the upward call of God in Christ Jesus. (3:12–14)

The Holy Spirit of God is pointing to the finished work of Christ in the sanctuary, in the streets, in the stadiums as we proclaim the gospel and persuade others to repent and believe in Him.

In this account of his conversion, we see Christ's apprehension of Paul when he was separated from God and brought into the true knowledge of the gospel. What clearer text can we have to show that Jesus Christ is pursuing sinners, that Jesus Christ came into this world seeking to save that which was lost, and that He pursues and apprehends those who were His enemies to redeem them and bring them into His fold?

Jesus Christ apprehended Paul on this road to Damascus, and it was a life-changing experience. The Holy Spirit of God is the Spirit of Christ, and He is testifying of Christ and pointing to the finished work of Christ in the sanctuary, in the streets, in the stadiums as we proclaim the gospel and persuade others to repent and believe in Him. Right now, Jesus is seated at the right hand of God the Father in His glorified resurrection body interceding for us. He has sent His Spirit to apprehend those who need to be convicted of sin righteous in judgment so that they may give their lives to Jesus Christ.

Finally, the third word or observation is *transformation*. This was a life-changing experience for Saul. His name became Paul, but that was the least significant change in his life. You can have a name change and not have a nature change. Here we find a man who was a God hater, who was under the wrath of God, yet believed that in his religious conviction and passion and zeal, he was doing God a favor, that he had a corner on God's market. Yet, he was fatally wrong. Had Jesus Christ had not apprehended him, had Saul not come to Him through this account on his travel to Damascus, he would have forever been on the way to hell.

Transformation means being born again by the gospel. The rest of chapter 9 details how God instructed Paul to find Ananias in Damascus. Ananias baptized Paul by his profession of faith in Christ. Paul called upon the name of the Lord and believed on Christ. According to the New Testament, God sealed him as a child of God and commissioned him to be the apostle to the Gentiles. You see, God called Saul to become Paul and to die to himself and go forth as a transformed person, a sinner now saved by grace, to be used as an earthen vessel to declare the gospel to the known world at that time. He was to reach the unreached people groups in his generation. Oh, dear friend, God is able to take any sinner, no matter how reprobate or rebellious, and through the apprehending gospel of Jesus Christ, He can pluck those souls from the fire and display them as trophies of grace, so that they may go and declare to the nations, across the street and around the world, that Jesus Christ saves. Would you join me in taking this conquering gospel to those in the marketplace who need to be born again like Saul?

God bless you, my friend.

DAY 28

· · ✦ ✦ ◆ ✦ ✦ · ·

Now behold, two of them were traveling that same day to a village called Emmaus, which was seven miles from Jerusalem. And they talked together of all these things which had happened. So it was, while they conversed and reasoned, that Jesus Himself drew near and went with them. But their eyes were restrained, so that they did not know Him.

Luke 24:13–16

*B*eginning with Luke 24:27 we find this:

And beginning at Moses and all the Prophets, [Jesus] expounded to them in all the Scriptures the things concerning Himself. Then they drew near to the village where they were going and He indicated that He would have gone farther. But they constrained Him, saying, "Abide with us, for it is toward evening, and the day is far spent." And He went in to stay with them. Now it came to pass, as He sat at the table with them, that He took bread, blessed and broke it, and gave it to them. Then their eyes were opened and they knew Him; and He vanished from their sight. And they said to one another, "Did not our heart burn within us while He talked with us on the road, and while He opened the Scriptures to us?"

Well, dear friend, here we see the context of the Lord Jesus walking along the road to Emmaus beside these two disciples.

Now, this was Resurrection Sunday. This was Easter Sunday in the evening. It was the day Jesus was raised from the dead. This chapter is a narrative of this seven-mile walk between Jerusalem and a town called Emmaus. I want to share three observations with you that flow out of these verses I've read within the context of the entire chapter 24.

First is the word *expectations*. Now, these two disciples were walking to Emmaus. They had lost hope and were in despair. You see, they had trusted in Jesus of Nazareth to be the Messiah to the Jews. They expected Jesus to come and establish a military or political power in Israel to restore Israel to its great time of prosperity and power—just as when King David reigned in Jerusalem. They witnessed Jesus crucified on Friday and saw him buried in the tomb. Now they see an empty tomb and cannot understand the truths that Jesus had prophesied about himself. They had failed expectations. Dear friend, have there been expectations in your life? Maybe within your workplace, your family, or your career ambitions that have not turned out exactly the way you intended? I think we can all relate to these two disciples in some way. When we have failed expectations, it can feel like we have been in a train wreck and have no idea how to move forward. This is how these two disciples felt on that first Easter Sunday. And they had Jesus Christ walking with them seven miles along that road and could not see it was Him. So even though the disciples' expectations were dashed, soon within their spiritual sight, they would see. The expectations they had were so little compared to what God was doing in bringing redemption and salvation to Israel and the whole world.

The second observation is the word *conversation*. Notice that these two men were talking to Jesus for seven miles. They are walking, and Jesus was obviously an excellent listener. He listened to these two men talk about all the events of the prior week. They shared many things. These men recalled the last week, the Passion Week, when Jesus, of course, was delivered by the high priest to Pilot and crucified as a criminal on a Roman cross. This conversation went on, and the two men talked while Jesus continued to listen. I want to share this truth with you today. There are many days in my life, and I'm sure in your life, when things do not go as we planned. We might be talking to family or friends or looking for counsel with other people. That's a wonderful thing, and the Bible encourages it. But listen, the greatest listener of all for you and I today is the Lord Jesus Christ. Many times, we don't even realize that He is with us wherever we go. He will never leave or forsake us. These two men on that road did not understand that who they were talking to was the very hope for their salvation. Their greatest dreams could not come close to what God had done on that Easter morning when Jesus Christ raised from the dead. In the spirit of holiness, He came out of that tomb. He thereby defeated sin and death in the grave. These men had a conversation, and Jesus listened, but the time was coming when Jesus would then expound to them the things of Himself concerning the Scriptures. Can you imagine those two men at the point when they started hearing from Jesus about the prophets, Moses, and all the Old Testament writings? They had learned the Old Testament, and they knew all of that, yet when they were listening to Jesus expound from the Scripture the

Many times, we don't even realize that He is with us wherever we go. He will never leave or forsake us.

things concerning Himself, they had the Living Word of God shared with them. These two men were no doubt taking it in, and something happened. They began to realize that this man had great authority, which leads us to the third observation.

We see the word *illumination*. The Scripture says they stopped at the disciples' house, and Jesus came in. There, when Jesus broke the bread and blessed it, something happened. Do you know what happened? The spiritual light bulb came on. Everything they heard on that seven-mile journey, as Jesus expounded on the Scripture and taught them about the prophecies of Christ, came together. They began to understand Christ had to suffer and die for their sins and the sins of the world and then be raised in glory. All of that was coming together. And when Jesus blessed them in that moment, they had spiritual eyes, and they could see that their expectations were nothing compared to what God had done through the deliverance of the Jews and the Gentiles from their sins through the work of Jesus Christ. And so, Jesus disappeared physically at that moment. But for the first time, these men had spiritual sight. It was twenty-twenty vision.

Paul prayed for the Ephesians to be enlightened and that their eyes would be opened so that they may see the riches of the glory of God, the glorious gospel of Jesus Christ, and the hope they have through Christ. And so, illumination is simply when God commands the light to go into darkness. God did it at creation. And I tell you, every time someone comes to faith in Christ and embraces Christ in a saving way through repentance and faith, God commands the life of the gospel to shine in the darkness of man's heart. These two men were forever changed on the road to Emmaus because they had a personal encounter with Jesus Christ.

Dear friend, in the marketplace that we travel, there are times for conversations about Jesus. Yes, there are gospel conversations that ask about Christ or the purpose of life or discuss comparative religions. You and I have the opportunity, like Jesus, to listen to what they are saying and then respond with the Word of God, speaking the truth in love. We can be the mouth of Christ and share the glorious gospel, and I tell you God's Spirit will work. God has said, where there is sowing, there will be reaping. By the grace of God, those in the marketplace in darkness, can be illuminated and born again by the gospel. May it happen through your life and mine today as witnesses.

God bless you, my friend.

DAY 29

· · ✦ ✦ ✦ · · ·

Then the kingdom of heaven shall be likened to ten virgins who took their lamps and went out to meet the bridegroom. Now five of them were wise, and five were foolish. Those who were foolish took their lamps and took no oil with them, but the wise took oil in their vessels with their lamps. But while the bridegroom was delayed, they all slumbered and slept.

And at midnight a cry was heard: "Behold, the bridegroom is coming; go out to meet him!" Then all those virgins arose and trimmed their lamps. And the foolish said to the wise, "Give us some of your oil, for our lamps are going out." But the wise answered, saying, "No, lest there should not be enough for us and you; but go rather to those who sell, and buy for yourselves." And while they went to buy, the bridegroom came, and those who were ready went in with him to the wedding; and the door was shut.

Afterward the other virgins came also, saying, "Lord, Lord, open to us!" But he answered and said, "Assuredly, I say to you, I do not know you."

Watch therefore, for you know neither the day nor the hour in which the Son of Man is coming.

Matthew 25:1–13

I direct your attention to the book of Matthew chapter 25, verse 1. Here we find Jesus teaching a parable during His Mount Olive discourse.

Here we find Jesus teaching a parable. The context here was Jesus teaching His disciples about the end days and those things that would come. A parable is simply an earthly story with a heavenly meaning. And so Jesus was focusing on the second coming. Do you realize today that Christ will come again, and that the only promises in the Word of God that have not been fulfilled are those surrounding the second coming of Christ? Oh, dear friend, He came the first time to save, and He is coming to judge the second time. There are three observations or words that I want to describe flowing out of this parable.

First of all, the word *responsibility*. Notice there were ten virgins. This was a setup for a Jewish wedding, so these ten virgins were a part of the wedding party. When the bridegroom came, they would be there with the bride. What happened was out of the ten, only five were really ready. There were only five that were expecting his return and prepared for his return. There were five who were physically there within the crowd if you will. But they had not prepared. They were slothful and had no oil for their lamps. When the bridegroom came, there needed to be oil for the lamps to provide light for the wedding party. The responsibility was very clear. Five virgins were successful in their assignment of preparation for the bridegroom's coming, and five failed their assignment. Are you listening today? As twenty-first century Christians, you and I have a great responsibility to expect the second coming of Christ and prepare for it.

Oh, you and I can be in churches, and we can even participate in external religious acts. We can participate within the Assembly of God, the church of the Firstborn visibly, and we can sing out and hallelujah and amen. But dear friend, if you and I are not

We can sing out and hallelujah and amen. But dear friend, if you and I are not born again by the gospel of Jesus Christ, we are no different than these five foolish virgins.

born again by the gospel of Jesus Christ, we are no different than these five foolish virgins who would find that judgment was coming because they rejected the revelation and the Word of God.

Today in the marketplace, so many are going about their daily activities. Many are going about their lives even as professing believers, but they have never been possessed by the gospel and never truly trusted Jesus by faith. Oh, friend, today may we share the gospel with others, and may we proclaim that the king is coming. He is the bridegroom. He has come once, but He is coming again to receive His people, and the responsibility of followers of Jesus Christ is to be obedient to His Word to live by the gospel and seek Him while He may be found.

The second word is *urgency*. Did you notice when the midnight cry came announcing the bridegroom was coming, there was a time of chaos, wasn't there?

The five foolish virgins had panic attacks. If you ever have one of those, they're not fun. When these virgins realized they had not properly prepared, there was an urgency to find oil for their lamps. They were procrastinators. Oh, hear me today, dear friend. Today is the day of salvation. God is saving sinners today in the marketplace. He is using His church, His visible people in Great Commission efforts worldwide, and He is doing it not just in the third world countries but right here in The United States of America. He's doing it not just within the church walls but also in the highways and the byways. He is doing it among communities all around our country when His people proclaim the gospel of Jesus Christ. The Word of God will not return void. That is the urgency today that we face really as believers and followers of

Christ. We that we must proclaim His message, but there is also an urgency for unbelievers today. That is they should seek the Lord while He may be found today. If you are outside of Christ, oh dear friend, seek the Lord right now and flee from the wrath to come. Call upon the Lord Jesus Christ for whosoever shall call upon the name of the Lord Jesus shall be saved.

Dear friend, this can happen right now in your life if you trust in Christ. For those who are born again believers and committed followers of Jesus Christ who are listening today, the urgency is that those outside of Christ are not prepared for his second coming because they have never received him the first time. What a glorious opportunity we have to be witnesses for Jesus Christ!

The third observation, another word I've chosen—the word *finality*. Now there came the time when the five foolish virgins went into the market to get oil for their lamps, and while they were gone, the bridegroom arrived. It is very, very similar to those parables Jesus taught where He would come like a thief in the night, and there will be two walking down a road, one will disappear, and one will be left. There may even be a husband and wife in bed, and the husband will be gone or the wife will disappear because one is a believer one's not. There may be two in the board room, and when Christ comes again, there'll be a finality. And listen, the door of salvation will be shut. That's right. The door will be shut.

This seems so harsh to many, and why didn't He just open up. We were a little late. Do you remember when Noah built his ark, and his family went into the ark. After one hundred years, that preacher of righteousness was there, and finally, God sent rain for the first time. You remember the Scripture says those same words, *and the Lord shut the door*. The Lord shut in Noah's family—those who believed in God by faith and were justified by faith. Noah and the eight in his family, were shut in the ark by God.

Those outside perished because they rejected the Word of God that Noah had proclaimed to them for a hundred years. There was a finality. Here we see a finality with these foolish virgins. The door was shut. Oh, dear friend, today as we close, we must know this season of grace has an open door. It is an open door for whoever believes on the Son, whoever believes in Jesus. It does not matter their profession. It does not matter their education level. It does not matter where they came from or what their family of descent. Dear friend, today that door is open for anyone who will come by way of the cross. Hear me, in this parable, there is a warning. There is finality coming, a day when mortality will stop, and those outside of Christ will be judged. They will be left outside the door. The door of heaven will close.

Would you join me in taking the gospel to the ends of the earth? Would you join me in praying that God would prepare divine appointments in gospel conversations so that others may hear the gospel and be saved?

God bless you, my friend.

DAY 30

····✦✦✦✦✦✦····

God be merciful to us and bless us,
And cause His face to shine upon us, Selah
That Your way may be known on earth,
Your salvation among all nations.

Let the peoples praise You, O God;
Let all the peoples praise You.
Oh, let the nations be glad and sing for joy!
For You shall judge the people righteously,
And govern the nations on earth. Selah
Let the peoples praise You, O God;
Let all the peoples praise You.
Then the earth shall yield her increase;
God, our own God, shall bless us.
God shall bless us,
And all the ends of the earth shall fear Him.

Psalm 67

I direct your attention to Psalm 67 in the Word of God. Here we find a Psalm, often called the missionary psalm or the Psalm of the Great Commission. I would like to share three observations that are true today for us in the marketplace as we take the gospel of Jesus Christ to the ends of the earth. You and I, as believers, have been commissioned. We are to take the gospel of Christ and make disciples to the ends of the earth. This is our commission from the Lord Jesus Christ.

Here is the observation I would like to flow from the context of this Scripture. *God's heart is upon the nations.* In verses 1–3, Scripture tells us God has blessed us. He has been merciful to us through His free gospel of grace. Friend, you understand that today if you are a born-again believer, you were not looking for God. God found you. God did not choose you because of your righteousness or merit or because of something you have done. You came to Christ because Jesus pleases the Father in His righteousness given to you. The wages of sin is death, but when you repent of your sin and trust in Christ, the gift of God is eternal life. This is the spiritual blessing we have. And this blessing is not for us to sit and soak. As Dr. Adrian Rogers used to say, the spiritual blessing is to be a blessing to other people. In other words, God has blessed us with salvation so that we can be a blessing to others and a blessing to the nations. We are a blessing to them by making the way of God known and proclaiming His salvation among all nations. Do you realize today that God's heart is upon the nations? Do you realize today that in God's providence, He has assigned a time for people or groups to live within a location, within boundaries, and to have earthly governments? He ordained this from before the creation of the world. Do you realize His heart has been on the nations? It was there from the blessing to Abraham in Genesis, through the sea, and to the Lord Jesus Christ in the flesh. It is for all the nations. The gospel is for every nation and for every marketplace. The gospel is for every person. And through the heart of God, it throbs.

I have a picture in my study that I look at often. It depicts the earth within a large heart, and that heart is a picture of God's heart for the world. The Bible says in John 3:16, "For God so loved the world that He gave His only begotten Son, that whoever believes in Him should not perish but have everlasting life." The heart of God throbs for sinners from every people. And so here we are today, in the 21st century, the people of God, commissioned to proclaim the gospel to the nations in those marketplaces of activity around the world. But listen, God has brought others to our country, and our country is now a melting pot of many ethnicities. May our hearts throb today, just as Christ's heart throbbed for all the nations and every race. May we have the heart that God has for the world.

The gospel is for every nation and for every marketplace. The gospel is for every person. And through the heart of God, it throbs.

The second observation is *God's hand is upon the nations.* Notice in verse four the Scripture says, "Oh, let the nations be glad and sing for joy! For you shall judge the people righteously, and govern the nations on earth." Today, I want you to know that God's sovereign hand is upon the nations, and it is God who raises up earthly leaders. Their heart is in the hand of God, no matter how pagan, no matter how God hates it. We even see this with Nebuchadnezzar in the time of Daniel. We see God's hand working through history. This is providence, God intervening and interacting within human affairs. God is not a deity who is like a clockmaker in the sky who set the earth in order and then became passive. God is actively working, according to His counsel, His will and the gospel of grace, extended to all the nations. And so, we see a sovereign direction. We see though there is unrighteousness in this world today, God is the righteous one, the judge of the earth. He is the one who is governing the nations. He is calling out men, women, boys, and girls from their countries and homes through the gospel of Jesus Christ. God is sovereign, and He is working in this way for the redemption of sinful men.

The last observation is *God's harvest is with the nations*. Notice the Scripture says, "the earth shall yield her increase; God, our own God, shall bless us." Well, here is that blessing coming again. The blessing we received when we were saved. We are seeing there will be an increase. Many interpret this as the millennial period where Christ comes again and rules and reigns for a thousand years. There will be a literal, material, and physical yield like never before, like the pre-fall in the Garden of Eden. I believe this is true.

But listen, I believe it also has a spiritual sense. I believe in the Kingdom of God advancing today with the gospel in the Great Commission. As Christ's church arises and takes the gospel to the nations, God's harvest is with the nations, and we see people come to faith in Christ. Today, they have renounced idols, other gods, and false religions, and they come to true faith in Jesus Christ. They repented of their sins and have been born again by the gospel of Christ. Today, in our generation, God is granting an increase of gospel fruit found in every nation around this world. Do you realize that in one generation, dear friend, in a marketplace, a nation, and a platform, that the gospel cannot lose its influence? We can look back now and see the carnage in history among former evangelical nations and countries and communities. We can see now that they are against the Bible in terms of understanding it is God's revealed inspired word. All things can change quickly. How can this change if we are not out in the marketplace, and out proclaiming the gospel of Christ? How can it change if we are not practicing the gospel of Christ or teaching and making disciples? Oh, you say that sounds hard and rigid for the believer. But this is the greatest joy that you and I could ever experience—to be servants of the Master, to witness the harvest of souls that God is bringing up. Scripture tells us that faith comes by hearing and hearing by the Word of God. God's harvest is with the nations. I am not talking about material prosperity, but I am talking about soul prosperity. "The earth shall yield her increase." Today, we pray that God will use us to bring thirty, sixty, and one hundred full-gospel fruit. Are you willing to come alongside us? I pray that you are a member of a Bible-believing church, and that you are active in your devotion and your declaration of Christ. But dear friend, today is the time. God's harvest is with the nations. His hand is upon the nations and His heart is upon the nations.

God bless you, my friend, as you go in the marketplace proclaim the gospel.